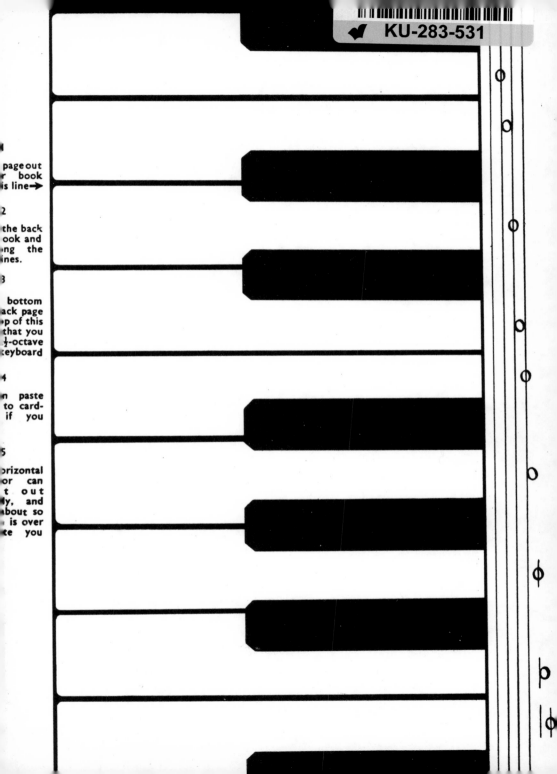

page out
book
is line→

2

the back
ook and
ng the
ines.

3

bottom
ack page
p of this
that you
½-octave
keyboard

4

n paste
to card-
if you

5

rizontal
or can
t out
ly, and
bout so
is over
te you

RAY"	SOH'
DOH"	FAH'
TE'	ME'
LAH'	RAY'
SOH'	DOH'
FE'	TE
FAH'	TAW
ME'	LAH
RAY'	SOH
DOH'	FAH
TE	ME
LAH	RAY
SOH	DOH
FE	TE,
FAH	TAW,
ME	LAH,
RAY	SOH,
DOH	FAH,
TE,	ME,
LAH,	RAY,
SOH,	DOH,

A GRADED MUSIC COURSE FOR SCHOOLS

BOOK TWO

A GRADED
MUSIC COURSE
FOR SCHOOLS
BOOK TWO

ANNIE O. WARBURTON
Mus.D., L.R.A.M., A.R.C.M.

LONGMAN

LONGMAN GROUP LIMITED
London

*Associated companies, branches and representatives
throughout the world*

First published 1956
Thirteenth impression 1974

ISBN 0 582 32587 0

Printed in Hong Kong by Peninsula Press Ltd.

NOTE TO THE TEACHER

This, the second book of the " Graded Music Course " has the same aims and continues on the same lines as Book I.

Everything in the scheme of work is suited to the age of the 12-13 years old. But only the best classes, with a generous music time-table, will be able to work through the book in its entirety. It was thought better to offer too much material than too little, as the teacher can then adapt or omit as he or she thinks fit, without being at a loss for examples or exercises. All classes should cover the ground of the main scheme, but those with less time might, for example, omit the harder sightsinging examples, deal only briefly with intervals and chords, do less original work or less " appreciation ".

On the language side this book deals with semiquavers and the pattern ♪♫ , compound time and its more common time patterns; the keys of D and B♭ major, as well as further work in C, G and F; chromatic notes, fe and taw; modulation from a major key to its dominant major and back; intervals of the 2nd, 3rd and 4th; the primary triads, and the cadences using them; and simple melody writing.

The study of the minor key has been left until Book III, as the notation is so complicated. But the essential aural differences between major and minor are dealt with, in a general way, in this book, without any reference to different methods of sol-fa usage.

On the literature side the book deals with the dance forms, and minuet and trio, episcdical, variation and rondo form, including comments on the sonata as a whole; the instruments of the small classical orchestra; and the composers Purcell, Bach, Haydn, Chopin and Brahms.

The sightsinging examples given in this book should form the nucleus of the sightsinging material used, as they are carefully graded, illustrative of each new point and give practice in time patterns which have been learnt, as well as in pitch. But, by the end of chapter II, enough knowledge has been gained for it to be possible to use any other sight singing or song books, containing easy examples in the keys concerned, that the school may happen to possess. Some classes will need a larger number of easy exercises than there was room to include in this book. The more difficult exercises given here can be omitted, if desired, without upsetting the scheme.

The Somervell shorthand has again been used. Somervell suggests treating $\frac{6}{8}$ as 6 quaver beats, so that, e.g. ♫♫♩. becomes | | | ⌐ . The author feels, however, that it is psychologically sounder to continue to call the beat taa, and give the sign " | ", whether it is written as ♩ , ♩ or ♩. . Some teachers may feel that, by this stage, shorthand has served its purpose, and may, therefore, prefer not to use it in compound time. For those who feel it can still be useful the author suggests some new signs for patterns in compound time. A complete list of time patterns and their shorthand equivalents used in this book is given on p. x.

A cut-out keyboard has again been included at each end of the book, though it is not on cardboard. It can be pasted on to thicker material, if wished. The modulator is complete on a separate page, so it can be used without necessarily cutting it out.

Whereas in Book I it was found necessary to write special examples to illustrate points in the language section of the book, the widening musical knowledge of the pupil at this stage makes it possible to use many examples from traditional tunes or from the works of the great composers for this purpose in Book II. Accordingly, the teacher will find a close correlation between the language and literature sections of the book. Examples used for musical form, musical instruments and composers are also closely correlated. They have been chosen from works which are recorded, but a wide selection has deliberately been given, so that teachers may be able to use one or other of them according to what they have available.

The quotations consist of the melody only, as this is all that the class can perform, as a class. But it is to be hoped that the teacher will usually play the accompaniment at the same time, so that the class gets pleasure from singing them, and is able to recognise the themes when they are heard in the complete work.

A list of quotations and references is appended; but it should be realised that some quotations, which illustrate a point in language, may be taken from a work which is not suitable for hearing in its entirety at this stage—e.g. a theme from a Brahms symphony; while other works, such as Chopin's " Revolutionary " study, which are not suitable for quotation, may be very suitable for hearing as a complete work.

QUOTATIONS AND REFERENCES

* = reference only

ACKNOWLEDGEMENTS

We are indebted to Messrs. Boosey & Hawkes Ltd. for permission to reproduce Purcell's tune *The Moor's Revenge* from *The Young Person's Guide to the Orchestra* by Benjamin Britten, and to the Church Music Society and the Oxford University Press for an extract from Robert Bridges's poem *Jesu Joy of man's desiring*.

CONTENTS

MUSIC LANGUAGE

MUSIC LITERATURE

CHAPTER VII

CHAPTER VIII

CHAPTER IX

TIME PATTERNS, WITH THEIR TIME NAMES AND SHORTHAND EQUIVALENTS

SIMPLE TIME

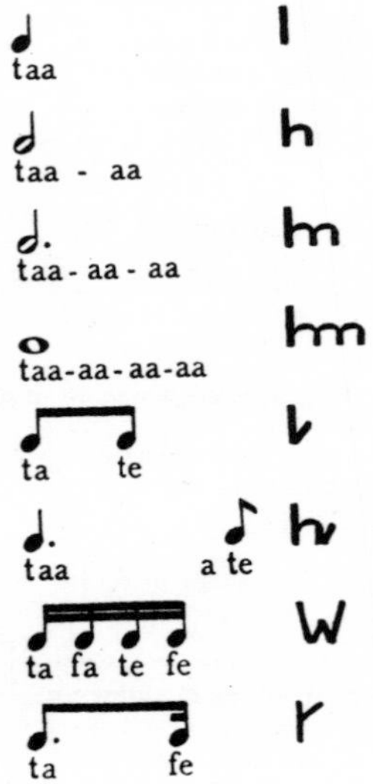

taa
taa - aa
taa - aa - aa
taa-aa-aa-aa
ta te
taa a te
ta fa te fe
ta fe

COMPOUND TIME

taa
or
taa-aa
ta te ti
ta (e) ti
ta te (i)
ta fe ti

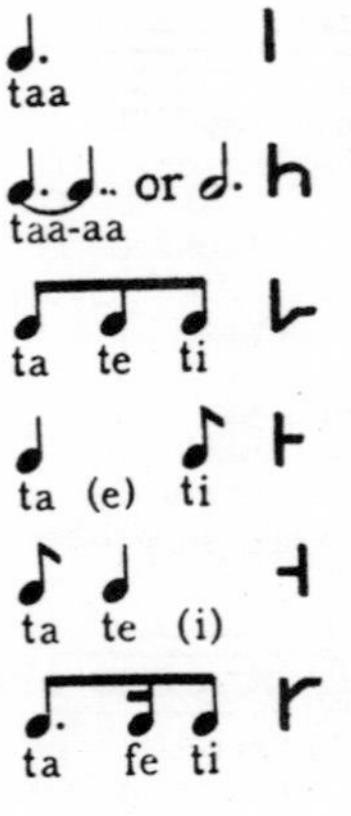

MUSIC LANGUAGE

Chapter One

THE TETRACHORDS OF A MAJOR SCALE. BUILDING A NEW SCALE FROM THE TOP TETRACHORD

A scale can be divided into two halves, each containing four notes. These halves are called *tetrachords*. In a major scale each tetrachord consists of two tones followed by a semitone.

Because the two tetrachords are exactly the same shape, it is possible for the top tetrachord (s l t d) of one scale to become the bottom tetrachord (d r m f) of another.

THE KEY OF D MAJOR

In the same way the scale of D major can be built from the scale of G major.

I

Cut out the two halves of the dummy keyboard at the end of the book and fasten them together. Then cut out the horizontal sol-fa chart above the keyboard. Now you can play the scales of C, G and D on the dummy keyboard, singing the pitch names at the same time. If you place the sol-fa chart with doh over C, G and D in turn, you will see for yourself that the semitones are in the right places.

The key signature of D major looks like this:—

The old English ballad, " Barbara Allen " is usually sung in the key of D. Learn it in sol-fa, and associate the sound of it with the key of D, to help you to remember the feel of the key.

Barbara Allen

Exercise 1. Staff pointing on the scale of D, entirely by step, class singing (a) sol-fa names; (b) fixed pitch names.

Exercise 2. Teacher sings a note to sol-fa in key D, class answers with its fixed pitch name, and vice-versa. Movement to be entirely by step.

Sight Singing, Key D, By Step

Exercise 3. Sing the following (a) to fixed pitch names; (b) to sol-fa. Play the tunes on the dummy keyboard at the same time.

THE DOH CHORD, KEY D

Exercise 4. Sing " The Trumpet Song " from Book I, in the key of D. Then write it out in this key.

Exercise 5. Staff pointing, key D, stepwise and using leaps to notes of the doh chord.

Exercise 6. Answering sol-fa names for pitch names and vice-versa, key D, using stepwise movement and leaps to notes of the doh chord.

SIGHTSINGING, KEY D, COMBINING DOH CHORD LEAPS WITH STEPWISE MOVEMENT

Exercise 7. Sing the following at sight:—

Exercise 8.   Pitch ear tests in the key of D.

Melodic and Harmonic Intervals

When a tune moves from one note to the next the intervals between the notes are called *melodic* intervals. But when two or more notes are sounded at the same time they make *harmonic* intervals.

Concords and Discords

Harmonic intervals are divided into concords and discords. A *concord* sounds pleasant and complete in itself. E.g.:—

A *discord* is harsher and always wants to move on. Some discords are harsher than others, but all have this tendency to move. The following are all discords. Could you put them in order of harshness? You may feel that one of them is quite pleasant—but it wants to move.

MAJOR AND MINOR SECONDS

You are doubtless familiar with the word " major " as meaning larger than " minor " When the interval of a second is a whole tone it is called a major second; when it is a semitone it is called a minor second.

All seconds are discords, but the minor second is harsher than the major. Play all the seconds in the major scale, to see if you agree.

Exercise 9. Learn the following song. It will help you to remember the sound of major and minor seconds.

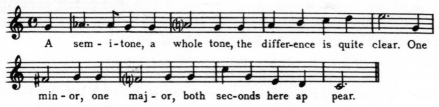

It has been said that the power to recognise the difference between a tone and a semitone is at the root of all good hearing ability. Learn the sound by singing, and then listen keenly.

Exercise 10. Sing a major second or a minor second above or below notes sung by your teacher.

Exercise 11. Ear tests. State whether seconds played by your teacher are major or minor.

When two notes making a second are meant to be performed at the same time (that is, when they make harmonic seconds) they are *not* written immediately above each other, but side by side. They are sometimes called " crushed " notes. You will see plenty of them in piano music.

Exercise 12. Copy the following.

All tones and semitones are not necessarily seconds. E to G♭, though a tone, is a kind of third, because three letter names are concerned, while F to F♯ is a kind of " first ". A second must consist of notes with adjacent letter names.

Exercise 13. Write (a) a major second above; (b) a minor second above; (c) a major second below; (d) a minor second below each of the following notes:—

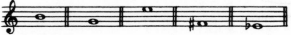

THE TRIPLET

Sometimes composers want to divide a beat into three equal parts. But unfortunately there is no note length which lasts for a third of a crotchet. It has become the custom, therefore, to write ♪♪♪ for three equal parts of a crotchet, and to call the group of notes a *triplet*. ♪♪♪ without the " 3 " would, of course, equal a dotted crotchet, but the " 3 ". by some sort of magic, is supposed to make three quavers equal two!

The time name of this pattern makes use of the next vowel after a and e, that is, " i ", thus:—tateti, pronounced French fashion—the time names were invented by a Frenchman, Aimé Paris. The suggested shorthand sign is ∟ . Practise writing this while you say tatetis.

Exercise 14. Divide class into two halves. One half clap the beats, and say taas; the other clap triplets and say tatetis. Class to change sides at the command of the teacher.

Here is a well-known tune in which the beats frequently divide into three. Try to hear it mentally before you sing it. Do you know its name? Learn it to time names. Then write the time pattern down in shorthand.

Exercise 15. Clap beats and then divide them up at the teacher's command, saying taas if he calls out " one ", tates if he calls out " two ", and tatetis if he calls out " three ".

SIGHTSINGING USING THE TRIPLET

Exercise 16. Sing the following:—

The following is part of a tune from Tschaikowsky's " Pathetic " Symphony. It is a rare instance of a piece of music in 5 time.

Tschaikowsky. *2nd movement Pathetic Symphony*

The following is the beginning of a famous chorale "Jesu, Joy of Man's Desiring", from a cantata by Bach. Strings play the triplet accompaniment, and at bar 9 the chorale tune (i.e. hymn tune) enters. Sing the string accompaniment and the chorale tune separately and then, with class divided into two, try to sing them together.

Bach. *Jesu, joy of man's desiring*

1. Je - su, joy of man's de - sir - ing,
2. Drawn by Thee, our souls as - pir - ing,

Ho - ly wis - dom, love most___
Soar to un - cre - a - ted___

bright.
light.

Exercise 17. Ear tests. 4 bar time patterns, including triplets

Writing a Short Melody from Dictation

In dictation tests you have written rhythmic patterns without pitch, and pitch without rhythm. Now you are to combine the two. You will probably find the pitch harder than the rhythm, so deal with that first. Work thus:—

(a) Write the sol-fa names above the staff.

(b) Write tiny dots, underneath the sol-fa names, on the right lines and spaces. Make them small enough to be turned into black or white notes later.

(c) Put in the bar lines next—and remember that "a bar line is a thing you *hear*". You may think it easier to get the note values first, and then add the bar lines to make the right number of beats in each bar, without listening for the strong accents. But if you have made a mistake in note values the bar lines will be wrong, too. It is far safer to put the bar lines in first—by *listening*. Anyone can hear a strong beat who really listens.

(d) Lastly, sing the tune to time names and turn the little dots into crotchets, quavers, and minims, etc.

Rests are very difficult to hear—in fact, there is often little or no difference between a minim at the end of a phrase and a crotchet followed by a crotchet rest. Bar 2, in Exercise 15 (h) would have sounded no different if Tschaikowsy had written ♩ ♩ ♩ 𝄽 . Rests are, therefore, not usually required in simple dictation tests.

Exercise 18. Dictation of easy two bar and four bar melodies.

TWO PART SIGHTSINGING

If two parts are written on the same stave the top part always has its stems up and the bottom part has them down. If a note has two stems, then both parts sing it. If two parts sing the same semibreve it is written **oo** . A part which is silent has rests, and if there is no room for them in the third space they are placed higher or lower, as convenient—even, possibly, using leger lines.

Exercise 19. Sing the following. In the first two examples the other part always sings your note just before you come in. The next two are *canons*, that is, the two parts are the same, but one enters after the other. Sing them in *unison* first (that is, both parts singing the same at the same time.) In (e) and (f) sing each part separately before trying them together.

Exercise 20. Additional exercises.

1.   Write the two tetrachords of the scale of F, marking the semitones. By building a new scale, based on the top tetrachord of the old, show how to move from F to C to G to D. What will the next scale be?

2.   Using treble and bass staves, write the key signatures and the tonic chords of the keys of F, C, G and D. Put the root of each chord in the left hand, and all three notes in the right.

3.   Name three pieces you have sung, played or heard, in the key of D. Then write the sol-fa name of the first note in each case.

4.   Write " Barbara Allen " from memory, in the key of D.

5.   Transpose " Barbara Allen " into the key of C.

6.   Copy " Oh, dear, what can the matter be " on p. 6 and write the sol-fa names underneath each note.

7.   Define (a) tetrachord; (b) melodic interval; (c) discord; (d) harmonic interval; (e) concord; (f) major second; (g) minor second; (h) crushed note; (i) triplet; (j) unison; (k) canon

8.   Play " Barbara Allen " by ear, on the piano or the dummy keyboard, in the key of D.

9.   Using the sol-fa names as a link between the two keys, play " Barbara Allen " in the key of F.

10.   Write exercise 7(h) in $\frac{4}{4}$ time.

11. Write exercise 7(i) in ²⁄₂ time.

12 By experimenting on the piano, write down two intervals which you think are concords, and two which are discords.

13. What is (a) a major second above F♯; (b) a minor second below G♭; (c) a minor second above C; (d) a major second below F; (e) a minor second below F♯?

14. Write a tune in the key of D, on this rhythm:—

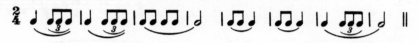

15. Copy the tune from Tschaikowsky's " Pathetic " Symphony quoted in exercise 16(h). Add the sol-fa names under each note. Then transpose it into the key of C, and play it in both keys.

Chapter Two

PRIMARY TRIADS, D MAJOR

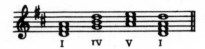

Sing " The Song of the Primary Triads ", from Book I, in the key of D. Then write it out from ear in the key of D.

SIGHTSINGING, KEY D, INCLUDING LEAPS ON I, IV AND V

Exercise 21. Sing the following:—

* These notes, which come in between the chord notes, by step, as a kind of decoration, are called " passing notes ". People sometimes sing additional unwritten passing notes in between chord notes. Two tunes where they are often wrongly added in this way are " O God our Help " and " O Come, all ye Faithful ". Sing through these tunes, and see if you can tell where these extra notes are sometimes slid in.

CHORD SINGING

The class, divided into three parts, sings the following. Bars 1, 3, 5 and 7 are sung in unison; each part goes to its own note in bars 2, 4, 6 and 8.

CADENCES. THE PERFECT CADENCE

A *cadence* is the name given to the ending of a phrase. Some cadence endings sound more finished than others.

The soh chord followed by the doh chord (V I) is the most common type of finished cadence, and you should learn to recognise it by ear. It is called a *perfect cadence.*

Exercise 22. Ear tests on recognising the perfect cadence, in comparison with other less finished cadences.

Exercise 23. Look at the Brahms tune on p. 36. Cadences occur in bars 5, 10, 14, 18 and 23. Name the last two notes of each phrase in sol-fa, and decide whether V I can fit under them, and thus make a perfect cadence. Then listen to your teacher playing it with the harmonies, and decide whether Brahms has used a perfect cadence in each of these places or not.

CHROMATIC NOTES

Revise the sol-fa names of the chromatic scale.

The major scale notes are usually sharpened, with their ending changed to "e" ascending; and flattened, with their ending changed to " aw " descending. An exception is " saw ", which is never used: " fe " is used both ascending and descending.

Here is the chromatic scale of G, built in the same way. Notice that taw is no longer a flat, but a natural.

Exercise 24. Write the chromatic scale of D, ascending and descending. Write the sol-fa names over the stave first, then the notes below. Use the dummy keyboard and the scale chart as a guide.

Chromatic notes, as their name implies, add colour to melody and harmony. There are rarely more than one or two in tunes, but in quick piano music, for example, you may find a complete chromatic scale. The chromatic scale is difficult to sing. Try it.

The most commonly used sharpened chromatic note is " fe ", and the most common flattened one is " taw ", but all of them are found at times. Mozart was particularly fond of decorating his tunes with chromatic notes. The following is the beginning of the slow movement of his " Prague " symphony.

Listen while your teacher plays it, then join in and sing it. Then work out what the sol-fa names are, and sing it again to sol-fa. Bars 6 to 8 make a complete chromatic scale, from fe, to fe.

Exercise 25. Sing the following. Name the chromatic notes before you start. They should help you to realise the difference between major and minor seconds, as they so often produce a minor second.

The next tune is the bass part to " Dido's Lament" from Purcell's opera " Dido and Aeneas ". The downward movement by semitones makes it sound very pathetic. Purcell repeats this bass continuously throughout the song, and has different melodies and harmonies making variations above it. This type of composition is called a " Ground Bass ". " Dido's Lament " is one of the greatest songs ever written, and it is available on gramophone records.

Purcell. *Dido's Lament*

MUSIC WRITING — NATURALS

Naturals are awkward to write and require practice. Make them in two parts, thus:— ⌐ and ¬ = ♮.

Exercise 26. Copy Exercise 25 (a).

COMPOUND TIME

A triplet, as you know, consists of three notes in the time of two.

 without the " 3 " above or below, obviously equals a dotted crotchet.

There are two ways of writing " Oh, dear, what can the Matter be ". The first way was shown on p. 6. Here is another:—

This method involves making a dotted crotchet the beat, but there is no reason why this should not be done. Any note length can be a beat. It saves the labour of putting " 3 " over or under every set of quavers, and it is the more common way of writing the tune.

If a composer wants all, or nearly all, his beats to divide into three, he will find it easier to make a dotted note for the beat. Dotted crotchets are frequently written as beats, because they can divide into three equal quavers.

When the beats of a piece of music divide into two it is said to be in *simple* time: when they divide into three it is in *compound* time. This has nothing to do with the *number* of beats in a bar; you can compose in simple two time, compound two time, simple three time, compound three time, and so on.

Simple two time:

Compound two time:

Simple three time:

Compound three time:

Learn these two rules:—

(a)   In simple time the beats are ordinary notes.
       In compound time the beats are dotted notes.

(b)   In simple time the beats divide into two.
       In compound time the beats divide into three.

Exercise 27.   Ear tests in recognising whether music played is in simple or compound time.   Clap the beats quietly, then say tate and tateti to yourself, inside each beat, and see which fits.   You must say the time names evenly, otherwise they are no test.

If you look at Chapter I, Exercise 16 (b), (c), (e), (f) and (g) you will see that sometimes the beats divide into two and sometimes into three, in the same piece of music.   When this happens you can please yourself whether you write with a crotchet or a dotted crotchet as a beat.   If you choose a dotted crotchet you will have to write a *duplet* (two notes in the time of three) when the beat divides into two, thus:— .   Exercise 16(b) was written like this:—

But it could have been written like this:—

They both sound the same, but in this case the first way is better, because it is less trouble to write.

Exercise 28.   Rewrite Exercise 16(e) and (f), with the beat as a dotted crotchet.

Exercise 29.   Sing the following at sight:—

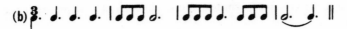

Exercise 30. Ear tests in compound time, using ♩, ♫♫ and ♩. only.

COMPOUND TIME SIGNATURES

In $\frac{2}{\text{♩}}$ time "♩" can be turned into "4", because, you remember, the bottom figure represents a proportion of a semibreve; there are four crotchets in a semibreve.

$$♩♩ = \frac{2}{\text{♩}} = \frac{2}{4} \qquad ♩.♩. = \frac{2}{\text{♩}.} = \frac{2}{?}$$

A dotted crotchet cannot be turned into a figure because it does not divide an exact number of times into a semibreve.

Let us try again

$$♩.♩. = ♫♫♫♫♫♫ = \frac{6}{\text{♪}} = \frac{6}{8}$$

Now we can turn a quaver into a figure, as there are eight quavers in a semibreve. So we get $\frac{6}{8}$. But unfortunately this is misleading, as although there are six *quavers* there are not six *beats*. $\frac{6}{8}$ is compound *two* time, containing two dotted crotchet beats in each bar.

Study the following, comparing the two sides of the table.

SIMPLE		COMPOUND	
♩ ♩ $= \frac{2}{\text{♩}} = \frac{2}{4}$	♩. ♩. $= \frac{2}{\text{♩}.} = $ ♩♫ ♩♫ $= \frac{6}{\text{♪}} = \frac{6}{8}$		
♩ ♩ ♩ $= \frac{3}{\text{♩}} = \frac{3}{4}$	♩. ♩. ♩. $= \frac{3}{\text{♩}.} = $ ♫♫ ♫♫ ♫♫ $= \frac{9}{\text{♪}} = \frac{9}{8}$		
♩ ♩ ♩ ♩ $= \frac{4}{\text{♩}} = \frac{4}{4}$	♩. ♩. ♩. ♩. $= \frac{4}{\text{♩}.} = $ ♫♫ ♫♫ ♫♫ ♫♫ $= \frac{12}{\text{♪}} = \frac{12}{8}$		
𝅗𝅥 𝅗𝅥 𝅗𝅥 $= \frac{3}{\text{♩}} = \frac{3}{2}$	𝅗𝅥. 𝅗𝅥. 𝅗𝅥. $= \frac{3}{\text{♩}.} = $ ♩♩ ♩♩ ♩♩ $= \frac{9}{\text{♩}} = \frac{9}{4}$		

Remember that $\frac{6}{8}$, $\frac{9}{8}$, and $\frac{12}{8}$ are the compound time equivalents of $\frac{2}{4}$, $\frac{3}{4}$ and $\frac{4}{4}$.

Of these $\frac{6}{8}$ is much the most common, and is the only kind of compound time we shall use this year.

Exercise 31.   Add time signatures to the following:—

Realise the difference between $\frac{3}{4}$ ♪♪♪♪ and $\frac{6}{8}$ ♪♪♪♪. Say them to time names and you will hear that the accents come in different places. In $\frac{3}{4}$ time a bar of quavers is often written thus ♪♪♪♪♪♪ , and occasionally this is found in $\frac{6}{8}$ time, too. In such cases you must look at the time signature to decide where the accents come.

MAJOR AND MINOR THIRDS

A major third consists of two tones; a minor third consists of a tone and a semitone. Play all the thirds in the key of C on the dummy keyboard, and you will see and hear that those containing me fah or te doh are minor.

Sing the scale of thirds, as shown above; then sing them without the intervening note; then half the class sings the top notes while the other half sings the bottom notes, thus:—

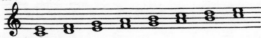

Then sing them in this form:—

Both major and minor thirds are concords, but minor thirds often seem weaker or sadder. Compare a major and minor third on the same note.

Learn the following, to help you to feel the effect.

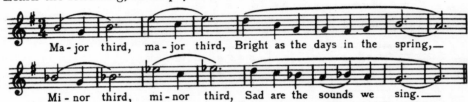

Ma - jor third, ma - jor third, Bright as the days in the spring,—

Mi - nor third, mi - nor third, Sad are the sounds we sing.—

Exercise 32. Write a major and a minor third on each of these notes:— A, C♯, B♭, E, A♭.

Exercise 33. Ear tests in recognising major and minor seconds and thirds.

You have already become familiar, in sightsinging exercises and ear tests, with d m and m s as parts of I, f l and l d' as parts of IV, and s t and t r' as parts of V. The only scale third you have not used is r f, and this is not difficult.

SIGHTSINGING USING THIRDS, IN UNISON AND TWO PARTS

Exercise 34. Sing the following:—

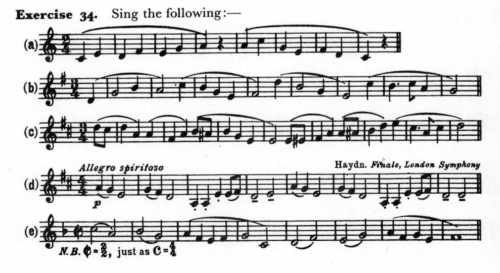

N.B. ₵ = ²⁄₂, just as C = ⁴⁄₄

COMPLETING MELODIES IN WRITING

When you compose a tune and like it, it is obviously an advantage to be able to write it down. Begin by singing the given opening phrase and then sing an answer, as you have done before. If you like what you have sung, sing it two or three times more, memorising it, so that it does not elude you when you start to write it down. Then write it down as if it were a dictation test, as shown in chapter I. You are really dictating it to yourself.

Exercise 35. Compose answering phrases to the following, and write down the complete tune. (Remember that phrases can begin and end in the middle of a bar.)

Exercise 36. Additional Exercises.

1. Using treble and bass clefs, write the primary triads in the key of D. Put the root of each chord in the left hand, and all three notes in the right.

2. Sing through " All through the Night " mentally and write down how many perfect cadences it has.

3. Define (a) cadence; (b) perfect cadence; (c) chromatic note; (d) simple time; (e) compound time; (f) major third; (g) minor third; (h) duplet.

4. Write a chromatic scale, ascending and descending, starting on F. Work as shown in Exercise 24.

5. Write the following notes on the staff in the keys of C, G, D and F:— (a) fe; (b) taw; (c) se.

6. Transpose Exercise 25(a) into the key of D. Write the sol-fa names first, as a bridge between the two keys.

7. Transpose Exercise 25(d) into the key of G.

8. Write " A Safe Stronghold ", given in Exercise 25(c) in $\frac{4}{4}$ time.

9. Sing ".Oh dear, what can the Matter be " to time names, writing it down in shorthand as you sing it. Transcribe it into notes, on one note. Write the sol-fa names under these notes, and from this write it out in the key of C.

10. Sing the following tunes to yourself and decide whether they are in simple or compound time, and how many beats in a bar they have. From this, write down their time signature:—(a) Hot Cross Buns; (b) Hickory, Dickory, Dock; (c) The Mulberry Bush; (d) The First Nowell; (e) Three Blind Mice.

11. Write the following in staff notation in key D:—

12.   What do the following time signatures represent?

(a) $\frac{2}{4}$; (b) $\frac{6}{8}$; (c) $\frac{3}{2}$; (d) $\frac{9}{8}$; (e) $\frac{4}{4}$; (f) $\frac{12}{8}$.

13.   Write (a) a major third above each of the following notes: A; E♭; B; F♯:· (b) a minor third above the following; C; F; B♭; C♯.

14.   Write out (a) all the major thirds in D major; (b) all the minor thirds in F major.

15.   Name the following intervals. (You can look at the keyboard, if you wish.)

16.   Copy the Haydn tune quoted in Exercise 34(d) and write the sol-fa names below each note. Then transpose it into the key of F.

17.   Memorise the tune from Haydn's " Clock " Symphony quoted in exercise 21(i). Then play it from ear.

18.   Look at the Haydn tune quoted in Exercise 34(d). Its shape consists of A B A B, with the last note of B changed at the end, to finish the tune off. A consists of a one-bar figure, repeated in the next bar a note lower, and thus making a sequence. Make a tune on the same plan. You can use the same rhythm if you like, too, but let your tune be in the key of G.

Chapter Three

MODULATION — ANOTHER ASPECT OF TONALITY

One of the best ways of getting variety in a piece of music is to change the key. Only the shortest and simplest pieces stay in one key all the time. Changing key in the course of the music is called *modulation*. Do not confuse it with transposition, the term used when the *whole* piece of music is put into a higher or lower key.

Listen while your teacher plays " Polly Oliver ".

Polly Oliver

Sing doh at the end of the first phrase, then again at the end of the second. You will realise you are not singing the same note each time. Then listen to the end, and you will realise it has returned to the first doh. However many times a piece of music modulates it always finishes in the " home " key—it would not sound finished otherwise.

Perhaps your teacher will play several versions of " Polly Oliver ", changing the second phrase so that it goes to a different key each time. Some modulations will sound better than others—in fact, some may sound very funny indeed! It all depends on their relationship to the first key. If the music moves to a key which has only one or two notes different from the first key it is rather like visiting your cousins, who are not so very different from yourselves, and we say it has moved to a *related key*. Other keys feel more distantly related, while key changes which involve changing most of the notes may feel as unrelated to each other as an Englishman does to a Chinaman!

Modulation is another aspect of tonality. Just as the notes of the major scale group themselves round doh and are drawn, as if by a magnet, to it, so different keys group themselves round the doh key. These are the related keys.

MODULATION TO THE DOMINANT AND BACK

Sing the following, while your teacher plays it.

You can see and hear it begins and ends in key C, but if you sing doh at bar 8 you will realise it has changed to key G. This is not surprising, for you already know there is only one note in key G which does not occur in key C (F♯), so the two keys are closely related.

Soh (G) has become the new doh. The musician's name for soh is *dominant*, so we say the music has *modulated to the dominant*. Where did it happen? About bar 7? In some pieces the change is gradual, in others it is sudden. In this tune there is a quick return to key C in bar 9. You will find a great many tunes that modulate to the dominant and back—in fact, it is the most common modulation of all.

Now look at the sol-fa names written over the tune. If you sing bars 7 and 8 with both sets of names you will hear that the key G names sound right and the key C names wrong—the last note does not feel at all like soh. But at bars 9 and 10 the key C names feel right again.

Notice also the use of fe (F♯) in key C, which becomes te in key G. It is no longer a chromatic note, because it belongs to the key of G. A note which belongs to the key is called *diatonic*. In bar 9 taw (F♮), a chromatic note in key G, becomes fah, a diatonic note, in key C. Fe and taw are often used to change from one key to another in this way. But the re in bar 12 is still a chromatic note, used as a decoration, and does not change the key. Notes that move up or down by semitones rarely change the key.

You may wonder what has caused the change of key. The use of F♯ instead of F♮ means, of course, that Haydn is using the scale of G instead of C for these two bars, but the harmonies, too, have a great deal to do with it. You will learn more about this later. The important thing is that your sense of tonality should make you able to hear where it has occurred.

Look again at " Polly Oliver " and by singing sol-fa names in keys C and G see if you can tell where the modulation takes place, and where the music returns to key C. It stays in the dominant key for longer than does the Haydn tune.

IMPLIED MODULATION

Sing " The Vicar of Bray ", using both sets of sol-fa names where they are given.

You will agree that the key G names sound right in the third phrase, and that the tune has modulated. There was no F♯ however this time—but neither was there an F♮. The composer just did not happen to use any kind of F in his tune at all in these four bars. But an F♯ is needed in the harmonies. If your teacher played it with harmonies in the key of C you would at once say that it was wrong. When an accidental is not used in a tune which modulates we say the modulation is *implied*.

SIGHTSINGING INCLUDING MODULATION

Sometimes a change of key only lasts for a few notes, and you may feel it is not worth changing the sol-fa names for so short a time. In the Haydn tune quoted above you may end the second phrase with the names d' d' fe fe s. But realise, all the same, that the key has changed. The more musical you are, the more difficult you will find it to sing the sol-fa names of the wrong key. It is, therefore, usually wise to change the names if the music is in a different key for more than a bar or two.

Exercise 37. Sing the following to sol-fa names, changing the names at the places shown. In (a) the modulation is so short that you can keep the sol-fa names of the key of C throughout, if you wish. Sing (d) to words or sol-fa names or both.

Ford. *Since first I saw your face*

Since first I saw your face I re-solved to ho-nour and re-nown you,
If now I be dis-dained I__ wish my heart had ne-ver known you.

What I that loved and you that liked, shall we be-gin to wran-gle?

No, no, no, my heart is fast and can-not dis-en-tan-gle.

MODULATOR AND STAFF POINTING INVOLVING MODULATION

Look at the modulator at the beginning of the book. You will see how, in changing from tonic to dominant key, soh becomes doh, lah becomes ray and so on. Fe of the doh key becomes te of the soh key, while, on the return journey, taw of the soh key becomes fah of the doh key.

Exercise 38. Point (a) "Polly Oliver", (b) the tune from Haydn's "Surprise" symphony, (c) "The Vicar of Bray", and (d) "Since first I saw your Face", on the modulator, changing key at the appropriate places.

Exercise 39. Teacher points tunes on the modulator for the class to sing, involving a change to the dominant key.

Now compare the scales of C and G.

Exercise 40. Point (a) "Polly Oliver", (b) the tune from Haydn's "Surprise" symphony, (c) "The Vicar of Bray", and (d) "Since first I saw your Face", on the two scales, as shown above, changing key at the appropriate places.

Exercise 41. Teacher points tunes on the staff, as shown above, involving a change to the dominant key, while class sings.

Exercise 42. Ear tests, class stating whether a tune (a) stays in one key, (b) modulates to the dominant key, or (c) modulates to some other key.

♩ ♪ AND ♪♩ IN COMPOUND TIME

Here are three ways in which a dotted crotchet beat can be split, in compound time:—

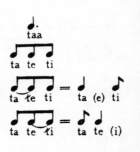

The time-names are self evident. The first two divisions are very common indeed: the third one is quite rare. ♩♪ has a skipping effect, while ♪♩, with the accent on the shorter note, sounds more like a lame man hobbling along! Clap each pattern several times, saying the time names, in order to feel the difference. Realise that ♩ in simple time is usually the beat, while ♩ in compound time is ⅔ of a beat.

Exercise 43. Teacher points to patterns on the above table, class claps whatever he points, while saying the time names.

Here is a tune using ♫♪, ♩♪ and ♩.

The Mulberry Bush

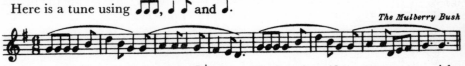

Here is another, which uses ♪♩ also. Notice that if a tune starts with a quaver before a bar line, in ⅜ time, the last note of the phrase will probably be ♩.♩, in order to make two or four complete bars.

The Two Magicians

Sing both these tunes to time names.

Suggested short hand signs:— ♩ ♪ = ┝; ♪♩ = ┥

Practise writing these, while saying the time names.

Exercise 44. Sing " The Mulberry Bush " and " The Two Magicians " to time names, writing them down in shorthand at the same time.

Exercise 45. Sing the following to time names. Your teacher may help you by playing the tune in (g), as it contains intervals you have not yet learnt.

Gay. *"Cease your funning" from "Beggar's Opera"*

Exercise 46. Teacher dictates four bar time patterns in compound time, using ♩♩♩, ♩ ♩, ♩ ♩, ♩., and ♩·

ITALIAN EXPRESSIONS MARKS SIMILAR TO ENGLISH

Learn the following:—

Grave	Grave, solemn	Animato	Animated
Largo	Large, broad, slow.	Grazioso	Gracefully
Vivace	Vivacious, with life	Marcato	Marked
Ad libitum	At liberty, as you please	Sostenuto	Sustained
Affettuoso	Affectionately	Tranquillo	Tranquil
Agitato	Agitated	Vigoroso	Vigorously.

TUNE WRITING IN COMPOUND TIME

Exercise 47. Copy the following beginnings, and write down an answering phrase in each case:—

THE IMPERFECT CADENCE

As you already know, some cadences are more finished than others. Unfinished cadences very often end with V, the soh chord, and these are called *imperfect*. Many different chords can be used before the V, though I is quite common. At an imperfect cadence you feel you can pause and take a breath, but your sense of tonality tells you that it is not the end of the piece. Look at the Bach Minuet in G on p. 32. There is an imperfect cadence at bar 8, but when this first section is repeated, it ends with a perfect cadence. Compare the two.

Exercise 48. Ear tests in recognising perfect and imperfect cadences.

MAJOR AND MINOR TRIADS

You know that a triad is a chord containing a root, third and fifth. A major triad has a major third from the root, while a minor triad has a minor third. Listen to the difference.

Exercise 49. Sing or play the following triads, and decide, by ear whether they are major or minor. Then check, by naming the kind of third between the two bottom notes.

MAJOR AND MINOR SCALES, OR MODES

The essential difference between a major and minor scale is that the major has a major third from its tonic, while the minor has a minor third. C major begins like this and its tonic chord, I, is a major triad, While C minor begins like this, and its tonic chord, I, is a minor triad . It will be seen that the first, fourth and fifth notes, upon which we build our primary triads, I, IV and V are the same in both cases.

There are three variants in the top half of the scale, and the notation of the minor scale is illogical and complicated, so further consideration of it is being left until Book III. In the meantime you should be able to tell whether music is in a major or minor key by listening to the tonic chord. Music in the minor mode is usually, but not always, sadder and more plaintive than that in the major. Listen to the National Anthem, and " Auld Lang Syne " played first in the major and then in the minor, and you will realise the difference. Of course a quick, vigorous tune sounds quite bright in the minor, but it would be brighter still if it were played in the major. " Charlie is my darling " is an example.

Exercise 50. Ear tests in recognising whether music is in the major or the minor mode.

MODULATION FROM G MAJOR TO D MAJOR

Modulation from G major to D major is another example of modulation to the dominant key.

Compare the two scales, noticing the links between the two, and the notes which make the chromatic sounds, fe and taw.

Sing the following while your teacher plays it. Sing an octave lower where necessary. Notice the effect of the modulation to the key of D.

Bach. *Minuet in G*

Exercise 51. Learn the following to sol-fa names. When you know it, point it on the double modulator at the beginning of the book, and on the two scales shown above.

Gathering Peascods

Exercise 52. Sing the following to sol-fa names. In the last two the changes
are not shown. Decide for yourself where they should come.

Exercise 53. Additional Exercises.

1. Look at the tunes quoted in Chapter VII, and see if you can find any
instances of modulation to the dominant.

2. Play " Ye Holy Angels Bright " on the piano by ear in the key of C.
Then write it down, showing where the changes of key occur.

3. Define (a) modulation; (b) dominant; (c) modulation to the domi-

nant; (d) related key; (e) diatonic; (f) implied modulation; (g) imperfect cadence.

4. Transpose " The Vicar of Bray " p. 26. into the key of D. When transposed, what key does it modulate to, in the third phrase?

5. What is the sol-fa name of the chromatic note which is used to modulate from the tonic to the dominant key? What is the fixed pitch name of this note when the tonic key is (a) C; (b) G; (c) F, and what key does it lead to in each case?

6. What is the sol-fa name of the chromatic note which is used to return from the dominant to the tonic key? What is the fixed pitch name of this note when the dominant key is (a) G; (b) C; (c) D, and what key does it return to, in each case?

7. Say the words of " Humpty Dumpty " to time names, in $\frac{6}{8}$ time. Then write the rhythm down in shorthand and transcribe it on one note.

8. Write the rhythm of " Little Miss Muffit " in $\frac{6}{8}$ time, working as in question 7. Then write a tune to it.

9. Suggest suitable speed and expression marks to be put at the beginning of the following tunes, all of which come in this chapter. Use the musical terms given in this chapter, as far as possible. (a) Polly Oliver; (b) the tune from Haydn's " Surprise" Symphony; (c) Since first I saw your Face; (d) The Mulberry Bush; (e) the tune from Beethoven's violin concerto; (f) the tune from Haydn's 'cello concerto; (g) Cease your funning; .(h) Bach's Minuet in G; (i) Gathering Peascods.

10. (a) What is the difference between a major and a minor triad? (b) what is the chief difference between a major and a minor scale?

11. State which of the following tunes are in the major, and which in the minor: (a) John Peel; (b) Oh, the Oak and the Ash; (c) Jesu, lover of my soul; (d) Ye Banks and Braes of Bonnie Doon; (e) The Ash Grove; (f) Three Kings of Orient (tune, not chorus).

12. Copy the Bach Minuet in G quoted in this chapter, trying to hear it as you write. Then add suitable phrasing and expression marks throughout. It is a dainty minuet, so it will require some staccato dots. Bach was not in the habit of writing expression marks on his manuscript, he would have expected you to be able to add your own.

Chapter Four

PRIMARY TRIADS ARRANGED FOR THE PIANO

There are many ways of writing primary triads for the piano. There are seven octaves in which you can play a chord, and ten fingers with which to play them! And if you play the chord melodically you can roam all over the piano at will, making *arpeggios*—so called because harps (Italian " arpa ") play that way. Try playing about with C E G all over the piano, using a mixtures of tunes, chords and arpeggios, and making two or four bar phrases. It is surprising what can be done with even one chord.

There is one way of playing piano chords which is very frequently used, and is easy to write. It is to play the root with the left hand, and one of each note in the right hand " in close position "; that is, as close together as possible. This makes three possible positions for each chord, thus:—

Chord I has been added at the end in order to finish with a perfect cadence.

Exercise 54. Play the primary triads, as shown above, in the key of C. Look at the book as you do so, noticing how you move from one position to the next.

Exercise 55. Write the primary triads, as shown above, in the keys of G, D, and F. Write in this order:—(a) the clefs and bar lines; (b) the roman numerals under the staff; (c) the bass notes throughout; (d) the first chord in the right hand with the root as the bottom note; (e) put the bottom note of the right hand an octave higher for the second position and repeat the process for the third; (f) treat the chords IV and V similarly; (g) finish with I, arranged so that te at the top of the previous chord rises a semitone to doh.

Exercise 56. Play the primary triads in close position in the keys of C, G, D and F. Start with the left hand and build up in the same way as you wrote

35

them. Never let go of one chord until you have thought out what you are going
to play next.

BUILDING A NEW SCALE FROM A BOTTOM TETRACHORD

Look again at the first two paragraphs in Chapter I of this book, which
showed how to build a new scale starting with the top tetrachord of an old one.
As the two tetrachords of a major scale are exactly the same shape, it is just as
possible to build a new scale downwards, starting with the bottom tetrachord
of an old one, thus:—

THE KEY OF B♭ MAJOR

This brings you to a new key—that of B♭ major. Its key signature is
Play this scale on your dummy keyboard.

Learn the following tune to sol-fa names, and link
it with the sound and feel of the key of B♭.

Exercise 57. Staff pointing on the scale of B♭, entirely by step, class singing
(a) sol-fa names; (b) fixed pitch names.

Exercise 58. Teacher sings a note to sol-fa in key B♭, class answers with its
fixed pitch name and vice versa, movement to be entirely by step.

SIGHTSINGING, KEY B♭, BY STEP

Exercise 59. Sing the following (a) to fixed pitch names; (b) to sol-fa.
Play the tunes on the dummy keyboard at the same time.

THE DOH CHORD, KEY B♭

Exercise 60. Sing " The Trumpet Song " from Book I in the key of B♭.
Then write it out in this key.

Exercise 61. Staff pointing, key B♭, stepwise and using leaps to notes of the
doh chord.

C

Exercise 62. Answering sol-fa names for fixed pitch names and vice versa, key B♭, using stepwise movement and leaps to notes of the doh chord.

SIGHTSINGING, KEY B♭, COMBINING DOH CHORD LEAPS WITH STEPWISE MOVEMENT

Exercise 63. Sing the following :—

Brahms *Waltz No. 8 etc.*

Exercise 64. Pitch ear tests in the key of B♭.

MORE MUSICAL TERMS

Learn the following:—

Adagio	slow	Maestoso	Majestic
Cantabile	In a singing style	Presto	Very quick
Dolce	Sweetly	Sotto voce	Under the voice— quietly
Espressivo	Expressively	Stringendo	pressing on
Leggiero	Lightly	Subito	suddenly
Lento	very slow	Tenuto	held, sustained

SEMIQUAVER NOTES AND RESTS

Semiquavers are, as their name implies, half as long as quavers. Therefore, when the beat is a crotchet, they last for a quarter of a beat. A single one is written thus: ♪ ; when there are four together they are usually grouped thus:— ♫♫ The first and third notes have the same time names as a pair of quavers, because they occur at the same points within the beat; the second and fourth notes, being lighter, use a softer consonant " f ", while keeping their correct vowel:

ta te

ta fa te fe

Exercise 65. Class divides into three parts, A representing crotchets, B quavers, C semiquavers. Each part claps its own note values, separately or together, at the command of the teacher, saying the time names.

Exercise 66. Class claps beats, while saying the time names of ♩, ♫, ♫♫ , or ♫♫ , according to whether the teacher calls out 1, 2, 3, or 4.

Semiquavers are not often used in tunes, as they are too quick to be easily singable. Haydn uses them, however, in this quick, gay movement. Sing it to time names, the first violin part an octave lower, the second violin part as written, and the 'cello part an octave higher. If you are lucky enough to possess a record of it, you will enjoy singing it with the quartet players.

Presto
Violin I   Haydn. *Finale String Quartet in C, op. 33 No. 3 "The Bird"*

Semiquavers are often used as decorations. Here is the beginning of the first variation on the Emperor's hymn from Haydn's " Emperor Quartet ". Sing the tune, which you know, while your teacher plays the semiquavers above it.

This also brings in the semiquaver rest— ⁊

Haydn. *Variation I, Emperor's Hymn, Emperor Quartet op. 76 No. 3*

The shorthand sign for  is ⋎ . Practise this, while you say the time names.

Exercise 67. Sing the tune quoted above from Haydn's " Bird " Quartet, and write it down in shorthand at the same time.

Sightsinging Using Semiquaver Notes and Rests

Exercise 68. Sing the following to time names:—

(d)

(e)

Beethoven. *1st movement of Sonata op 2, No.2*

(f)

r l

In (g) Brahms has written 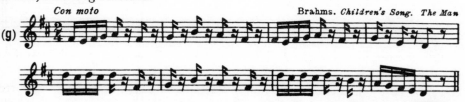, which sounds the same as . Call it tate, and sing staccato.

Con moto

Brahms. *Children's Song. The Man*

(g)

Exercise 69. Dictation of four bar time patterns incorporating

THE PRIMARY TRIADS, KEY B♭

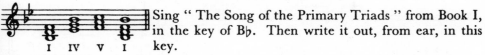

I IV V I

Sing " The Song of the Primary Triads " from Book I, in the key of B♭. Then write it out, from ear, in this key.

Exercise 70. Write the primary triads in key B♭ in close position for piano, three positions of each chord, as shown at the beginning of this chapter. Then play them without looking at your writing.

SIGHTSINGING, KEY B♭, INCLUDING THIRDS, AND LEAPS ON I, IV AND V

Exercise 71. Sing the following:—

(a)

I_____ V_____ I __ IV___ V __ I

Exercise 72. Additional Exercises.

1.   Play the scale, followed by the **primary triads** as shown at the beginning of this chapter, in all the keys you know.

2. Play the tune given in exercise 71(a) on the piano. Then play it again, adding the correct bass note at every change of chord. Those of you who are good pianists may even try to play a chord underneath the tune in the right hand at these places. It would be easier to play the chord in the left, but it sounds too " growly "

3. Play the scales of Bb, F, C, G and D on the piano or dummy keyboard. Keep the last four notes of each scale down, then play them again as the beginning of the next scale.

4. As question 3, but working backwards, starting with D and ending with Bb. Play the scales downwards.

5. Copy the tune from Brahms's " Variations on a theme of Handel " quoted in this chapter, trying to hear it as you write. Then write the sol-fa names over each note. Then learn the tune to sol-fa names.

6. Name as many songs as you can which are in the key of Bb. Then write down the melody of the first phrase of one of them, stating its name.

7. Transpose the tune from Brahms's Waltz No. 8 quoted in exercise 63 into the key of C.

8. Suggest suitable speed and expression marks for the Brahms and Haydn tunes quoted in exercise 71 (e) and (f).

9. Find a suitable place to use each of the new expression marks given in this chapter in the song book you are using. State clearly where each has to come.

10. Learn the Beethoven tune quoted in exercise 68(f). When you know it from memory, write it down in shorthand and transcribe it on one note.

11. Sing the following to time names on one note. Then copy the tune and write the solf-fa names above each note. Finally sing it or play it on the piano.

Haydn. *Minuet from Military Symphony*

12. Define (a) arpeggio; (b) close position; (c) Bb major.

13.   Put the following notes and rests in order of their length, starting with the longest.   State the number of beats each lasts, if the crotchet is the beat.

14.   Copy this tune, which is built on the primary triads with the chords changing every bar. Write the sol-fa names above each note, and the roman numerals underneath each bar. Then decorate the tune with a few passing notes.

Chapter Five

MODULATION FROM F MAJOR TO C MAJOR AND BACK

Sing the following, noticing first where the modulations occur. Morley, who was a contemporary of Shakespeare, modulates to the dominant key twice in this tune. Learn the tune to sol-fa names.

Morley. *Now is the Month of Maying*

Exercise 73. Point "Now is the Month of Maying" on the modulator, changing to the dominant key and back at the appropriate places.

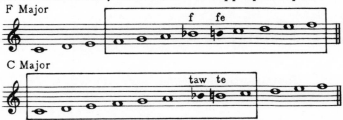

Exercise 74. Point "Now is the Month of Maying" on the scales of F and C major, shown above.

Exercise 75. Teacher points tunes on the scales of F and C major, involving modulation.

Exercise 76. Sing the following at sight:—

(b)

Amid the new mown Hay

WRITING AN EIGHT BAR TUNE ON THE PLAN A B A B^d.

The tunes you have written so far have all been four bars long. A longer tune nearly always contains some repetition. A simple plan for an eight bar tune is A B A B, with the first B unfinished (probably implying an imperfect cadence) and the second B changing at the end, so as to finish with a perfect cadence. When B is changed or developed thus we shall call it B developed, or B^d. for short.

Early One Morning

Exercise 77. Complete the following beginnings, to make eight bar tunes on the plan A B A B^d.

The most common time pattern using semiquavers is ♩. ♪ . Compare it with ♫ When singing or playing this time pattern take care that the second note is really short and lasts for only a quarter of a beat. Compare it with ♩ ♪ in compound time, where the second note lasts for a third of a beat.

Sing the following to time names, an octave lower than written.

Purcell. *Trumpet Tune*

Listen to your teacher playing Chopin's Prelude No. 7 in A, which is built entirely on ♩ | ♫♩♩ ♩ | ♩ ‖

The short hand sign for ♫♩ is ⌐ . Practise this while you say the time names.

Exercise 78. Sing Purcell's " Trumpet Tune " to time names and write it down in shorthand at the same time.

Exercise 79. Sing the following to time names:—

In writing time patterns from dictation, take care not to confuse 𝅘𝅥𝅮𝅘𝅥𝅮 and 𝅘𝅥𝅭 𝅘𝅥𝅮 . 𝅘𝅥𝅮𝅘𝅥𝅮 takes only one beat, while 𝅘𝅥𝅭 𝅘𝅥𝅮 lasts over two—you can feel the beat in the middle, taa-*ate*. Sing through Exercise 79(e) again, carefully noting the difference between the two patterns.

Exercise 80.   Dictation of four bar time patterns incorporating 𝅘𝅥𝅮𝅘𝅥𝅮 .

Note and Rest Groupings in Simple Time

Normally the notes belonging to the same beat are grouped together, as, for example 𝅘𝅥𝅮𝅘𝅥𝅮𝅘𝅥𝅮𝅘𝅥𝅮 and 𝅘𝅥𝅮𝅘𝅥𝅮 .   Compare   ¾ 𝅘𝅥𝅮𝅘𝅥𝅮 𝅘𝅥𝅮𝅘𝅥𝅮 𝅘𝅥𝅮𝅘𝅥𝅮𝅘𝅥𝅮𝅘𝅥𝅮 | 𝅗𝅥. ‖   with

¾ 𝅘𝅥𝅮𝅘𝅥𝅮𝅘𝅥𝅮. 𝅘𝅥𝅮𝅘𝅥𝅮𝅘𝅥𝅮𝅘𝅥𝅮 | 𝅗𝅥. ‖   . The first example can be said to time names and makes sense; time names do not " work " with the second, and it gives no indication of where the accents occur.

Notes of the same value may, however, be grouped together for the first or second half of a bar in four time, e.g.:   4/4 𝅘𝅥𝅮𝅘𝅥𝅮𝅘𝅥𝅮𝅘𝅥𝅮 𝅘𝅥𝅮𝅘𝅥𝅮𝅘𝅥𝅮 (but not 4/4 𝅘𝅥 𝅘𝅥𝅮𝅘𝅥𝅮𝅘𝅥𝅮𝅘𝅥𝅮 𝅘𝅥); or for a whole bar in triple time, e.g.: ¾ 𝅘𝅥𝅮𝅘𝅥𝅮𝅘𝅥𝅮𝅘𝅥𝅮𝅘𝅥𝅮. . Rests should show the divisions of the bar into beats in the same way.   E.g.: ¾ 𝄼𝄾 𝄿 𝄾 𝄼 is correct; ¾ 𝄼 𝄽 𝄽 𝄼 is incorrect.

The first or second half of a bar can be shown by one rest, however. E.g.:— $\frac{4}{4}$ ♩ ♩ ▬ but not $\frac{4}{4}$ ♩ ▬ ♩ .

You already know that a semibreve rest is used for a whole bar's rest, whatever the time may be.

Exercise 81. Correct the following:—

Exercise 82. Group the notes in the following, so as to show where the beats occur. Which version is easier to read?

Purcell. *Hark, the echoing air*

THE PLAGAL CADENCE

A *plagal* cadence is made by the chords IV I. It is just as finished as the perfect, but is much less common. IV has a " heavy " feel compared with V, so the cadence feels heavier and more solemn. For this reason it is frequently used for " Amen ".

In distinguishing between the cadences, decide first whether doh is the bass of the final chord (perfect or plagal), or whether it is soh (imperfect). If it is doh, then listen to the bass of the chord before, and decide whether it is soh (perfect) or fah (plagal). A check is to sing te doh while the last two chords are being played. They will fit if the chords are V I (perfect) but clash if they are IV I (plagal).

Two tunes that end with a plagal cadence are " Good King Wenceslas " and " Ye Banks and Braes of Bonnie Doon ".

Exercise 83. Ear tests on recognising perfect, imperfect and plagal cadences.

Perfect and Augmented Fourths

Two different sizes of fourths occur in a major scale, but they are not called major and minor as are the seconds and thirds. The normal-sized fourth is called *perfect* (your physics teacher may tell you why), and it contains two tones and a semitone. There is, however, one place in the major scale where three tones occur together—from fah to te. This, being a semitone larger than a perfect fourth, is called *augmented*. Another name for it is the *tritone*. It is awkward to sing, and the monks in the middle ages were forbidden to use it—in fact, they called it " the devil's interval !"

Sing the following to sol-fa names, noticing where the semitones come, and listening to the effect of all the fourths. Do you like " the devil's interval "?

Now sing a scale of harmonic fourths, dividing the class into two halves.

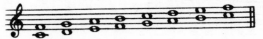

Was it as easy as singing in thirds? Do you like the sound as much? Do you think fourths are concords or discords?

You have already used d f as part of IV, r s as part of V, and s d¹ as part of I. Learn the sound of the other perfect fourths, m l, l r¹, and t m¹. You will rarely find the augmented fourth, f t, in a tune.

Exercise 84. Write a perfect and an augmented fourth on each of these notes, building up by tones and semitones:—C; A; D; E♭ F♯.

Exercise 85. Ear tests in recognising perfect and augmented fourths, first in isolation, then in comparison with major and minor seconds and thirds.

Exercise 86. Modulator pointing and sequence singing, using fourths.

Exercise 87. Name the following intervals:—

Exercise 88. Sing the following at sight:—

SINGING SONGS AT SIGHT

It is an obvious advantage to be able to read songs easily at sight. You can learn two or three times as many, and singing lessons are more enjoyable. Many people are lazy, however, when reading songs: they only look at the words. This is stupid, as a quick glance at the words is all you need, whereas the notes need much more attention. Even if the notation goes beyond your present knowledge you can grasp a good ·deal, and practice will improve your reading tremendously. So *always* look at the notes.

It was the custom, until recently, for notes sung to different syllables to have separate stems, even though they belonged to the same beat. This, however, makes it harder to see the beginning of each beat, and many publishers have recently decided to group the notes into beats, as in instrumental writing. If each syllable is put exactly under its own note or notes, it is easy enough to tell where it comes. Compare the old and new methods:—

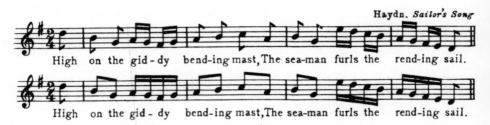

High on the gid-dy bend-ing mast, The sea-man furls the rend-ing sail.

High on the gid-dy bend-ing mast, The sea-man furls the rend-ing sail.

Brahms's " Cradle Song ", quoted below, is notated by the new method, and Haydn's " Sailor's Song " by the old. You need practice in the latter, as many of your school copies probably use it, but you will get plenty of song reading practice in the singing lessons. Put it to good use by looking at the *music*, not just at the words.

Exercise 89. Sing the following at sight:—

I know a love-ly land, I know a love-ly land, Where

food for all is al-ways free, And presents grow on ev-'ry tree, Where

all the peo-ple do a-gree, I know a love-ly land.

Sleep ba-by_ sleep. Thy Fa-ther guards his sheep. Thy Mother shakes the

dream land tree, Down falls a lit-tle dream for thee, Sleep ba-by sleep.

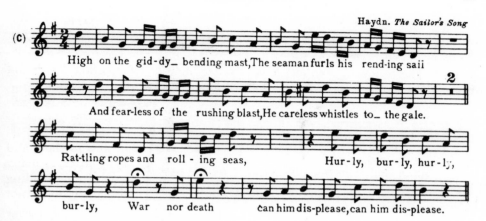

Haydn. *The Sailor's Song*

High on the gid-dy_ bending mast, The seaman furls his rend-ing sail

And fear-less of the rushing blast, He careless whistles to_ the gale.

Rat-tling ropes and roll - ing seas, Hur-ly, bur-ly, hur-ly,

bur-ly, War nor death can him dis-please, can him dis-please.

Exercise 90.   Additional exercises.

1.   Give the fixed pitch name of the note which has to be changed in order to modulate from F major to C major. What note is used in its place?

2.   Transpose Morley's " Now is the Month of Maying " p. 45 into the key of G. To what key does it modulate in the middle?

3.   Learn " Amid the New Mown Hay " p. 46 to time names. Then write it down in shorthand.

4.   Write the tune from Brahms's " St. Anthony Variations " twice as fast as it is written on p. 36, beginning thus:—
This is how Brahms wrote it.

5.   Write the rhythm of " Charlie is My Darling " or " The Minstrel Boy ", whichever you know best, in shorthand. Then transcribe it on one note.

6.   Correct the notational mistakes in the following. Do you know the name of the tune?

7.   Define:—(a) plagal cadence;   (b) perfect fourth;   (c) augmented fourth;   (d) the tritone.

8.—Write the Brahms song given in Exercise 89(a) in $\frac{2}{4}$ time.

9.   Learn the Brahms song given in Exercise 89(b) to sol-fa names. Then, by means of the sol-fa names, play it in the key of B♭.

10.   The following extract shows the old method of printing words and music. Write it out in the new way, showing the divisions into beats.

Part of Haydn's *"Mermaid's Song"*

Come and   I will lead the way   Where the   pearl - y   trea - sures be.

11.   Sing the following tune to time names and then to solfa names, and learn it by these means. Then write it out from memory, hearing it as you write.

Minuet from Mozart, *Quartet for flute and strings K.298*

Chapter Six

Each of the quavers in  can be divided into semiquavers. One rarely hears six semiquavers together in a tune, but several combinations of quavers and semiquavers are common. Study this table. The last of these patterns is the most common, so it is the first we shall add to our vocabulary of time patterns. Clap it while saying the time names.

Sing the following tune to time names, taking care to make ♩.♫♫ absolutely accurate. It is performed incorrectly more often than any other time pattern.

Suggested shorthand sign: **Γ** . (Be sure to move your pencil in time with the pattern.)

Sing " Sellenger's Round ", and write it down in shorthand. Then transcribe it on one note.

Exercise 91.   Sing the following to time names:

Exercise 92.   Dictation of four bar time patterns in ⁶/₈ time, including ♩. ♫♫

NOTE AND REST GROUPINGS IN COMPOUND TIME

Group notes so as to show the beats, as in simple time.   A two beat note may be written as ♩. ♩. or ♩   . .   A minim should never be used in ⁶/₈ time, as it represents a beat and a third.   If a tune begins with a quaver before a bar line the last note will probably be ♩. ♩   .

Rests should also show each beat.   The exception is the complete bar, which uses a semibreve rest, as in simple time.

Exercise 93.   Correct the following:—

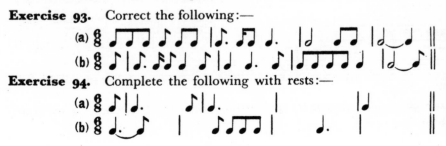

Exercise 94.   Complete the following with rests:—

MODULATION FROM B♭ MAJOR TO F MAJOR AND BACK

Here is a tune which modulates from B♭ major to its dominant, F major and back. Notice where the modulation occurs. Then sing it to time names (the stems are divided according to the syllables.) Then sing it to the words. Finally learn the tune to sol-fa names, and point it on the modulator.

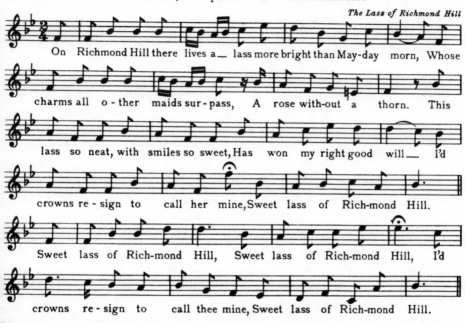

The Lass of Richmond Hill

On Richmond Hill there lives a— lass more bright than May-day morn, Whose charms all o - ther maids sur - pass, A rose with-out a thorn. This lass so neat, with smiles so sweet, Has won my right good will— I'd crowns re - sign to call her mine, Sweet lass of Rich-mond Hill. Sweet lass of Rich-mond Hill, Sweet lass of Rich-mond Hill, I'd crowns re - sign to call thee mine, Sweet lass of Rich-mond Hill.

Exercise 95. Point "The Lass of Richmond Hill" on the scales of B♭ major and F major, shown below.

Exercise 96. Teacher points tunes on the scales of B♭ and F major, involving modulation.

Exercise 97.   Sing the following at sight:—

The Roast Beef of Old England

(a)

When   might - y roast beef   was the   Eng - lish-man's food It   en

-no - bled our hearts   and en - rich - ed   our blood;   Our

sol - diers were brave,   and our   court - iers   were good

Oh   the roast beef   of   old   Eng   land,   And

oh   for old   Eng - lands roast   beef! _____

Haydn. *Minuet from Quartet op.1 No.1*

(b)

TUNE WRITING ON A B A C

Exercise 98. Write tunes on the plan A B A C, beginning as follows:—

THE QUAVER AS THE BEAT UNIT

You have, by now, met ♩, ♩, and ♩. as the beat unit. Composers occasionally use a quaver for this purpose also. It is sometimes found in songs, and in slow movements of sonatas and symphonies. Here is a list of note values, with their corresponding names, when the quaver is the beat:—

Taa-aa-aa-aa; taa-aa-aa; taa-aa; taa; tate; taa-ate; tafatefe; ta fe

You will feel this is confusing and be glad it is comparatively rare! Keep to ♩ in simple time, and ♩. in compound time when composing tunes, or writing from dictation.

Exercise 99. Sing the following to time names:—

Building Pieces with the Primary Triads

Study the following waltz, noticing how it is built up, with the primary triads in the bass, as chords, and the notes of the chords used melodically to make a tune in the right hand.

Exercise 100. Write a waltz in the key of C, using the same bass as in the example above, but with a tune of your own. Any note of the chord can be used in the right hand, in any order and any rhythm you think suitable. It is advisable to move mostly by step when changing from one chord to the next, otherwise your tune will have too many leaps.

Exercise 101. Write a march on the following chord scheme in the key of G:—I V I IV; IV I V I. Change the chords once a bar.

Exercise 102. Additional exercises.

1. The following is the rhythm of the beginning of a well-known English dance song. Can you name it?

2. Transpose "Sellenger's Round" p. 55 into the key of D. To what key does it modulate in the middle?

3. Write an eight bar rhythm for a maypole dance tune, starting thus:—. Then write a tune to this rhythm, in any key you like.

4.   Rewrite the following, correcting all the mistakes, and trying to hear it as you write. What is the name of the tune? Finish it, in correct notation.

5.   Rewrite "The Lass of Richmond Hill" p. 57 as it would probably be written in a modern edition. Take care to write each syllable in its exact place.

6.   Write the tune from Haydn's Clock Symphony, given in exercise 99, in $\frac{4}{4}$ time.

7.   Try to find a simple waltz, written for piano, in a key you have learnt. Mark all the places where you can find I, IV and V in the first section of the piece, by putting roman numerals under the bass.

MUSIC LITERATURE

Chapter Seven

MUSICAL FORM

THE DANCE FORMS

Music and dance have always been closely allied, and many musical forms owe their origin to dances.

In the days of Queen Elizabeth I people often danced on the village green to tunes such as " Gathering Peascods ", given on page 32 and " Sellenger's Round ", page 55. Folk dances such as these are still loved and danced to-day. The courtiers of Elizabeth I danced stately dances, such as the pavane and galliard. The pavane was in slow duple time, and the galliard was in quicker triple time, and they were usually put together to make a pair.

Sometimes composers wrote pavanes and galliards as instrumental pieces, not intended for dancing. But of course they were modelled on the style of the dance.

In the time of Bach and Handel, over a hundred years later, the idea of grouping dances together was extended. Four or more dances were put together to form a " suite ".

The *suites* were often written for harpsichords and clavichords, keyboard instruments which were invented before the piano, and which had quite a different tone. You may have heard them on the gramophone or the radio. Most of the dances were short, and every dance in the suite was in the same key. They were usually in binary form, with each half repeated. Dances which Bach and Handel liked to put into their suites were:—

(a) *The Minuet.* This had come from France, and was a stately dance in triple time. There are quotations from seven minuets in this book, on pp. 15, 32, 43, 54, 58, 68 and 81. Those by later composers, such as Haydn and Mozart, are usually a little quicker than those by Purcell, Bach and Handel. Here is the beginning of a lovely minuet by Bach, which will be found in " Dance Movements from Bach " (Paterson). You will be able to tell that it is in a minor key.

Bach. *Minuet from 2nd Suite for Orchestra*

(b) *The Gavotte.* This, too, was French, and was in ² time, with every phrase starting on the third crotchet in the bar. Here is the melody of the gavotte from Bach's French Suite in G. Notice that the first part ends in key D, the dominant key, and that the second part is longer than the first. This is often the case. The first part begins by leaping down in crotchets, while the second half leaps up in crotchets, thus developing the same idea.

(c) *The Musette.* This was a gavotte with a " drone " underneath, like that of a bagpipe, played on an instrument called a musette. It often followed a gavotte in a suite, and then the gavotte was played again, thus making a kind of large ternary form. There is a musette by Bach on p. 21. A drone G is played in the bass throughout.

(d) *The Bourrée.* This was like a gavotte, except that each phrase began on the last crotchet of the bar. Bach wrote one for solo 'cello beginning thus:—

It has been arranged for the piano in " Dance Movements from Bach ". If your teacher plays it to you notice that it is followed by a second bourrée in a minor key, after which the major one is repeated again. This lengthens the piece, just as the musette lengthens the gavotte.

(e) *The Sarabande*. This was slower and more stately than the French dances mentioned above. It was a Spanish dance, in triple time, and it often had an accent on the second beat of the bar. No. 5 in " Dance Movements from Bach " begins thus. Notice that it is another dance in a minor key.

(f) *The Gigue or Giga or Jig*. This was a quick, gay dance, in compound time, and it usually ended a suite. Although it is so often found in the works of Bach, a German composer, it is British in origin. There is a Scotch jig and an Irish jig. Will Kemp, an actor contemporary of Shakespeare, once danced a jig all the way from London to Norwich, for a wager! No. 7, in " Dance Movements from Bach " begins like this:—

Over a hundred years later, Chopin, a composer you are studying this year, also wrote dances. But he was Polish, so he wrote mazurkas and polonaises, which were Polish dances.

The Mazurka. This was a fairly quick country dance, in triple time. There was often a semiquaver at the end of the first beat, and an accent on the second beat of the bar. The beginning of No. 5 was quoted on p. 48. No. 14 begins like this. Its plan is A B : || C A ||. Although in a minor key, it is quite gay.

The Polonaise. This was more of a processional dance. It, too, was in triple time, but with the sections ending on the third beat. The first beat of the bar was often split up into shorter notes. E.g. . The first theme of Chopin's polonaise in C♯ minor starts like this:—

The first part is in C♯ minor, and the second part in D♭ major—can you see the connection? This piece is unusual, in that the first part does not return. Can you tell where the second part starts?

The Waltz. Chopin also loved the waltz, and wrote many waltzes for the drawing rooms of his friends in Paris. A waltz, as you are sure to know, is *written* in triple time, but perhaps you have not realised that it is often so quick that two bars of $\frac{3}{4}$ time really *sound* like one bar of $\frac{6}{8}$ time. Sing " The Blue Danube " while beating time to test this. Chopin's waltz in C♯ minor is, however, a slow one. Here are the themes A, B and C. Listen to it, and see if you can tell how it is built. It is not a very usual shape.

Brahms, who was born a generation later, also wrote waltzes, and as the dance originally came from Austria and as Brahms lived in Austria, this is not surprising. You may know the one quoted on p. 38. He also wrote vigorous and rhythmical Hungarian Dances which are often heard today. No. 5 is quoted on p. 95.

Exercise 103. Learn the definitions of all the dances mentioned in this chapter.

Exercise 104. By looking at the time signature, rhythmic shape, and speed of the following, name the kind of dances they are:—

Exercise 105. Write an 8 bar time pattern suitable for (a) a gavotte; (b) a gigue; (c) a minuet; (d) a bourrée. Then write a tune for one of the rhythms.

Exercise 106. Look at the *Radio Times*, to see if any of the dances mentioned in this chapter are being played during the week. Listen to any you can, and make a note of their name and composer.

SONATAS AND SYMPHONIES

When we come to the next pair of great composers after Bach and Handel, that is, Haydn and Mozart, we find them writing sonatas and symphonies instead of suites of dances.

A sonata is a large piece of music, usually in four " movements ", for one or two instruments.

A symphony is a sonata for orchestra.
A concerto „ „ „ „ solo (or solos) and orchestra.
A trio „ „ „ „ three instruments.
A quartet „ „ „ „ four „
A quintet „ „ „ „ five „ etc.

The dances of the suite did not altogether die out, however. Haydn loved the minuet, and usually wrote one for the third movement of his symphonies. But it seemed too short, in comparison with the other movements, so he added a second minuet, called a trio, to make it longer. It was called a trio, because originally it was often played by only three instruments, so as to make a contrast from the full orchestra. This is another meaning of the word " trio ".

MINUET AND TRIO FORM

The most usual plan for a minuet and trio is

MINUET   TRIO   MINUET
| A :||: BA :|| C :||: DC :|| A || BA ||

You will notice that although the minuet in this plan is in two parts, each part repeated, i.e. binary form, A returns after B in the second part, thus giving a feeling of ternary. This mixed form is sometimes called " hybrid form". Occasionally, however, the minuet or the trio or both are in a pure binary form A: ||: B: ||, without any repetition of A.

Notice also that, when the minuet returns after the trio, the sections are not repeated.

Sometimes there is a " link " between the trio and the return of the minuet, and sometimes there is a " coda ", to round off the whole movement at the end.

This plan is known as " minuet and trio " form, and it is used for other pieces, such as marches and waltzes. Chopin's Polonaise in A major is in this form.

Here are the beginnings of each section of the minuet and trio from Haydn's 'London Symphony".

If this piece is played to you, try to recognise each tune as it occurs. When A comes in for the second time, it is decorated. The trio is in a different key from the minuet, and Haydn uses a link to return to the minuet in the original key.

The second movement from Mozart's quartet in A major for flute and strings is also in this form. It is quoted on p. 54.

Episodical Form

The second movement of a sonata or symphony is usually slow. It often has a plan very like the minuet and trio, but without such obvious breaks at the end of each section, and without any repeats. The middle section, corresponding to the trio, is called an episode because it occurs only once, so the plan is called " episodical form ". The slow movement of Mozart's Clarinet Concerto is built on this plan. Here are the opening theme and the beginning of the episode:—

VARIATION FORM

Another common plan for the second movement (and sometimes for the first or last movement) is an air with variations. The slow movement of Haydn's string quartet "The Emperor" is an example of a variation movement. Here is the theme, which you know as a hymn:—

In the first variation Haydn gives the tune to the second violin, while the first violin embroiders round it. The beginning of this is quoted on p. 40. The 'cello has the tune in the second variation, while the viola plays a bass part below it and the two violins weave a decoration above it. Then the viola has a turn, with the other instruments weaving round it. Finally the tune returns to the first violin again, but has different harmonies, and after the first phrase it jumps an octave higher. There is a short coda, four bars long. You will easily follow this movement if you hear it on the gramophone.

The slow movement of Haydn's Surprise Symphony, whose theme is quoted as an example of modulation to the dominant on p. 25, is another air with variations. Perhaps you can hear this on the gramophone, too.

RONDO FORM

The last movement is very often in rondo form—A B A C A. The first theme, A, keeps coming round again, like a chorus. And it always returns in the same key, whereas B and C are in different, though related keys. Haydn's trumpet concerto ends with a rondo. The movement begins like this:—

Three other movements in rondo form, which you may get a chance to hear, are " Fear no danger to ensue " from Purcell's " Dido and Aeneas ", Schubert's " Entr'acte in B♭ " from " Rosamunde ", and Chopin's Mazurka No. 5. The song " Cherry Ripe " is also in rondo form.

D

Plan of a Symphony

First movement. Usually quick (Allegro), though it may have a slow introduction before the quick part. You will learn something about the form of this movement next year.

Second movement. Usually slow. May be in episodical form or variation form —or in other forms which you have not yet learnt.

Third movement. Often a minuet and trio, particularly in the works of Haydn and Mozart.

Fourth movement (finale). Usually quick and gay. Often in rondo form.

Exercise 107. Define the following, with as full a description as possible, and give an example of each:—(a) sonata; (b) symphony; (c) concerto; (d) quartet; (e) minuet and trio form; (f) episodical form; (g) rondo form.

Exercise 108. Look through any pieces you can play, to see if you can find an example of minuet and trio form, episodical form, or rondo form. Quote the main themes, and state the keys in which each section begins and ends.

Chapter Eight

INSTRUMENTS OF THE ORCHESTRA

The Wood-Wind Family

Last year you learnt about the instruments of the string family, instruments which are the foundation of the orchestra and which are used in much greater numbers than those of the other families.

The chief function of the wood-wind instruments is to provide contrasts of orchestral colour. There are usually two of each kind, and they often play two different parts, so that they are, in effect, solo instruments. The first of each pair usually has all the best tunes!

They are usually made of wood or ebonite, but you can have a flute made of silver and even of gold, if you are rich enough! They are all more or less tubular in shape, but there are differences about the shape of the inside hole—whether it is cylindrical or conical—which affect the tone of the instrument. A longer tube produces lower notes. The " keys " you can see on the picture cover holes. The air blown into the tube escapes through the first hole which is not covered. So, by uncovering each hole in turn, a player can produce a scale.

The Flute. This is easy to recognise at a concert because it and its little brother, *the piccolo*, are the only wood-wind instruments played sideways. Look at the picture. The player places the blow-hole *under* his mouth and then blows down into it—a tricky business! You have to have the right kind of lips and teeth to play a flute successfully! The lowest note is middle C, and very high notes can be reached. The flute has a soft, silvery tone, and can play runs very quickly. When Gluck wanted to give an impression of Elysium, the Greek heaven, in his opera " Orpheus ", he used a flute for the " Dance of the Blessed Spirits "

The German Emperor, Frederick the Great, played on a gold flute every night. But a court musician said of him " If you are under the impression that the King loves music, you are wrong. He only loves the flute—and, more than that, the only flute he loves is his own! " Perhaps this unkind comment was due to professional jealousy! However, the King later lost his teeth, so could not play any more, and from then onwards he lost all interest in music!

71

Flutes used to be very popular instruments in the home. Whole operas were arranged for them, and they were often used to accompany songs. They were popular in amateur orchestras, too. At one time, the orchestra of the " Gentlemen's Concerts " in Manchester had 26 flutes! But two is the usual number in a professional orchestra.

Mozart wrote a short and simple, but lovely quartet for flute and strings in A major. The minuet from this work is quoted on p. 54. The first movement is in variation form, and starts like this:—

The minuet quoted on p. 62 from Bach's Suite in B minor is also for flute and strings.

A recorder, which perhaps you play, is a kind of flute played downwards. Henry VIII not only composed for the recorder, he owned 76 of them!

The Oboe. This is another treble-sounding instrument, and it is about the same size as the flute. But it does not usually play as high or as fast, and its tone is plaintive and more " edgy ". When it plays quickly it can sound quite spiteful! In " Peter and the Wolf " Prokofiev uses the flute to represent the bird and the oboe to represent the duck, and this will help you to realise the difference in sound.

The oboe is played downwards, like the recorder. Two reeds, made from cane grown on the shores of the Mediterranean, are fastened together, and inserted in the mouthpiece. The player puts these in his mouth, and blows so that they vibrate against each other, producing what we call a " reedy " tone.

The oboe has never been as popular with amateurs as the flute and clarinet, perhaps because it is a little harder to play and more expensive to buy. But its tone in the orchestra provides a lovely contrast to the gentler wood-wind instruments. In Handel's day there were sometimes as many oboes as violins, but nowadays we are content with two.

Bach made use of the oboe. If your school possesses " The Columbia History of Music " you can hear the introduction he wrote to cantata No. 156, which

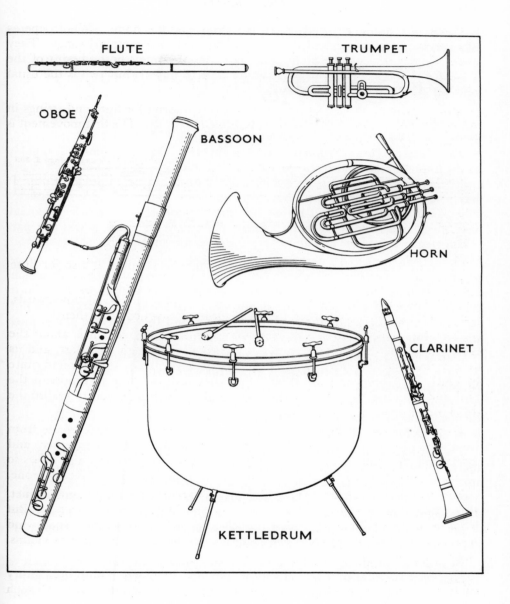

FLUTE

TRUMPET

OBOE

BASSOON

HORN

CLARINET

KETTLEDRUM

he called a " sinfonia ", and which is written for oboe and strings. It starts like this:—

Bach. *Sinfonia from Cantata No.156*

Lento

etc.

Handel wrote two fine oboe concertos, and Mozart wrote a quartet for oboe and strings, the last movement of which you would certainly enjoy.

The Clarinet. This instrument can play almost as high and almost as quickly as the flute, but it can also play nearly an octave lower. Its low notes can sound quite menacing, though its high notes can be mistaken for those of a flute. It has a rounder, fuller quality, however, and can " gurgle " very effectively! The lower notes can sound rather like the " mooing " of a cow! Prokofiev uses the clarinet for the cat, in " Peter and the Wolf" and marks the part " con eleganza ". One can almost see the sleek movement of a cat.

The clarinet is played downwards, like the oboe, and in the distance you may not be able to tell the difference. But the clarinet has only one reed, which makes the tone less reedy and edgy than the oboe, yet with more body to it than the flute. If you look at the picture you will see that the reed does not stick out at the top, as do the reeds of the oboe, and therefore the player puts the top of the instrument as well as the reed in his mouth.

Clarinets only came into use in the orchestra about the time of Haydn and Mozart. You were told in Book I how Mozart heard the instrument in the Mannheim orchestra, and fell in love with it. He wrote a clarinet trio, a clarinet quintet, and a clarinet concerto for a famous performer of his time. The themes of the slow movement of the concerto are quoted on p. 68. This, too, is in the Columbia History.

The Bassoon. Flutes, oboes and clarinets are all high-sounding, treble instruments. The bassoon is really a bass oboe, and the only one of the four which uses the bass clef. Like an oboe, it uses two reeds, though, being lower, it sounds less edgy. When it plays its higher notes it can sound " throttled ". Handel used it in his oratorio " Saul " to represent Samuel's ghost. Sometimes it plays rich 'cello-like tunes, and, on occasion, it can also sound comic. It represents the grandfather in " Peter and the Wolf".

In order to produce the low notes the tube has to be very long, but it is curved back on itself so that it is not too difficult to handle. The Italian name for it is " Fagotto ", because it looks rather like a bundle of faggots! A small curved tube connects the instrument with the reeds, so that they can more easily reach the mouth.

Mozart wrote a concerto for the bassoon. It has some lovely tunes, though the runs sound a little comic, particularly if you *see* the player at the same time! The last movement is a rondo, and begins like this:—

THE BRASS FAMILY

You have all heard a brass band, and you realise that the instruments are loud enough to " carry " in the open air. Some brass instruments are used also for the louder passages in the orchestra. They are always made of metal, though not necessarily brass, and you will be familiar with the curves and " bell " which they all possess.

Woodwind players produce a scale by opening and closing holes along the length of the instrument. But brass instruments are different. The players produce different notes by slackening and tightening their lips, and blowing in different ways.

The following notes are known as the " harmonic series ". (Your physics teacher may tell you why.) The series can start on any note.

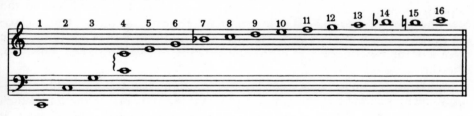

Brass players, starting on different notes, according to the size and shape of their instrument, can produce the notes of this series just by blowing in different ways. Bugle players can only produce from numbers 3 to 6, horn players can go up to number 12, while clever trumpeters can reach number 16, and so play a complete scale on their top notes.

When brass players want to play notes of a harmonic series starting on a different note, they have to lengthen their tube in some way.

The Horn. This is the quietest instrument of the brass section, and, therefore, it can even be used in quiet slow movements. It is also the most difficult to play. In Haydn and Mozart's day there were usually two horns in the orchestra, but nowadays there are usually four, and even sometimes six or eight. They are usually in pairs because each player trains his lips to play either the top or the bottom notes, but not both.

In Haydn and Mozart's day the players could only produce the notes of one harmonic series, unless they stopped playing for a while and added some extra tubing. So their tunes were very restricted, and largely built on chords. Nowadays they can move from one series to another by putting down " valves " —you can see them in the picture—which open some more tubes for the air to go through. So they can play any note within their range.

Although horn parts are written on the treble stave, the instrument has a middle range of notes, like that of a tenor or alto singer.

Horns can play a horn call—their ancestor was the hunting horn—but they can also play rich, soft chords, and they are good at playing slow throbbing repeated notes. Three horns play the part of the wolf in " Peter and the Wolf ".

To hear a horn concerto we will again turn to Mozart, who wrote four. Three are in the key of E♭, a good key for a horn. They all have three movements, which is usual for concertos, as they rarely have a minuet and trio. All four are quite short, and you would enjoy the second and third movements of them all. The last two movements of No. 3 begin like this:—

Brahms was a composer who loved writing for the horn (his father was a horn player). He wrote a horn trio, which you will enjoy when you are older, and also some part songs, with accompaniment for two horns and a harp, for a ladies' choir which he conducted in Hamburg.

The Trumpet. This is a very old kind of instrument—there were competitions in trumpet playing in the Greek Olympic games over 2,000 years ago! You all know what a modern trumpet looks like. Can you see the valves in the picture? They lengthen the tube the air passes through, as on a horn, and so produce a lower harmonic series. But the trumpet is higher and louder and more " brassy " than the horn. Haydn and Mozart used two in the orchestra, but to-day there are usually three.

It was not usual to use trumpets and drums in slow movements in Haydn's day, hence the surprise in the *andante* of Haydn's · " Surprise " symphony when they come in loudly in bar 16.

The trumpet is, of course, effective in trumpet fanfares which you have probably heard on special occasions. But it can also play noble tunes. There is a trumpet tune by Purcell on p. 47, and you may have heard the Trumpet Voluntary which it used to be thought was by Purcell, but is now sometimes attributed to Jeremiah Clarke. It begins like this:—

Allegro maestoso   Purcell? Clarke? *Trumpet Voluntary*

Handel wrote a trumpet part to accompany the aria " Let the Bright Seraphim " from " Samson ", and Haydn wrote a trumpet concerto. Its last movement is quoted on p. 69.

THE PERCUSSION FAMILY

Percussion instruments are mainly used in music with a story, and most of them cannot play a note of exact pitch. But the timpani or kettledrum can do so, and, therefore, it is very useful in symphonies. It is the only percussion instrument found in the orchestra of Haydn and Mozart.

The Timpani or Kettledrum. This consists of a pigskin stretched over a metal cauldron. Look at the picture. Can you see the taps round the edge? These are used to tighten or slacken the skin, and so alter the pitch.

In Haydn's day it was customary to use two, and they were tuned to doh and soh of the movement. They played single notes or time patterns or drum rolls. Nowadays there are usually three. The French composer, Berlioz, who lived 100 years ago, once wrote for 16, with 8 players, and in another piece he created a realistic thunderstorm by letting them play together in chords!

Timpani playing is not as easy as you might think. The player has to have very flexible wrists, and such a good ear that he can tune correctly even while music is being played. He also has to be very good at counting silent bars!

The timpani does not come through very well on the gramophone, though it is exciting to see and hear it at a concert. Drums play the rifle shots in " Peter and the Wolf ", with a trumpet solo in between each round.

Perhaps the clearest example of drums on the gramophone is in Britten's " Variation and Fugue on a Theme of Purcell."

THE SYMPHONY ORCHESTRA OF HAYDN AND MOZART

You have now learnt something about all the instruments used by Haydn and Mozart in their symphonies and concertos. Their orchestra was a small one by present day standards. It usually consisted of:—1 or 2 flutes; 2 oboes; 2 clarinets (but not in their earlier works, before the clarinet had come into regular use); 2 bassoons; 2 horns; 2 trumpets; 2 drums; and strings.

Many orchestral pieces by Haydn and Mozart have been referred to in this book, so you have probably heard enough to be familiar with the sound of their orchestra. Try to recognise each instrument when it plays the tune, as well as listen to the general effect.

Prokofiev's " Peter and the Wolf " uses all the instruments mentioned in this chapter as solo instruments, so it will help you to recognise them. But it is a modern work, written in 1936.

Britten's " Variations and Fugue on a Theme of Purcell ", the theme of which is quoted on p. 81, has, as its other title " The Young Person's Guide to the Orchestra ", and it, too, is helpful in learning to recognise the instruments.

Exercise 109. If you know anyone who possesses an instrument mentioned in this chapter ask for a demonstration of it.

Exercise 110. Next time you go to an orchestral concert try to distinguish all the instruments by sight before the playing starts, and then try to distinguish them by sound during the music, particularly when they play a solo.

Chapter Nine

COMPOSERS

PURCELL, 1658—1695

Purcell

Henry Purcell was an English composer who lived in " Good King Charles's Golden Days ", so he comes even earlier than Handel, who, you remember, came to England in the reign of George I. He is the greatest English composer between the reign of Elizabeth I and the twentieth century.

You probably know that Charles II was brought up in exile in France, while Britain was ruled by Oliver Cromwell. When he was restored to the throne, he brought many French ideas with him, and also a love of French music. So he sent one of his musicians, Pelham Humfrey, to France, to the court of Louis XIV, to learn the French ways of composing and performing music. When Humfrey returned he was put in charge of the boys of the Chapel Royal, to teach them in the way his master wanted, and among them was young Henry Purcell.

The Chapel Royal was a body of clergy, musicians and choir boys who provided a church service for the King every day, as well as various kinds of musical entertainment. Quite often they went about with him on his travels. They had a fine scarlet uniform, and the singers were often accompanied by 24 string instruments, just as in the court of Louis XIV.

Henry Purcell's father and uncle were both " Gentlemen of the Chapel ", and Henry himself early showed talent as a singer, so it was natural that he should join the chapel. There he was taught to play and sing, and he was soon composing too. When his voice broke he was kept on, looking after the musical instruments, doing much of the music copying that was necessary when so little music was printed, and later becoming organist of the chapel. At the

79

early age of 21 he was appointed organist of Westminster Abbey—a post for which he received £10 a year! He played for the coronations of James II and William and Mary. He wrote many anthems, some of which are quite gay, in the French style. He was fond of dotted rhythms, such as occur in his famous bell anthem " Rejoice in the Lord alway ".

But Purcell did not only compose church music. He often wrote music for plays that were staged in London theatres. Many of the songs you sing or hear to-day come from these plays. Can you name this one? Try to hear it in your head.

The following song comes from Dryden's play " King Arthur ", a play which has so much music in it that one might almost call it an opera.

Fairest Isle

Fair - est isle, all isles__ ex - cell - ing, Seat__ of pleas - ures
Ve - nus here will choose her dwell-ing, And__ for - sake__ her

and__ of loves, Cu - pid from his fav-'rite na - tion
Cyp - rian groves.

Care__ and en - vy will__ re - move, Jea - lou - sy that

poi - sons pas - sion And__ de - spair__ that sighs for love.

Another song, " Hark, hark, the echoing air " is quoted on p. 49, and you may have heard the exciting two part song " Sound the trumpet ". He also wrote music for a peculiar arrangement of Shakespeare's " A Midsummer Night's Dream," which was called " The Fairy Queen ". Someone else added words for the songs, and not one word of Shakespeare's did Purcell set!

Purcell wrote one real opera, to the story of " Dido and Aeneas ". It was written for a girls' school in Chelsea, run by a man called " Josiah Priest ". Purcell himself took part in it, but most of the other parts were taken by the girls. There are exciting parts in it for sailors and witches, and a jolly sailors' dance. A chorus sung by Dido's attendants begins like this and is in rondo form.

"Fear no Danger," from Dido and Aeneas

Fear no dan-ger to en-sue, The he-ro loves as well as you.

Just before Dido throws herself on the funeral pyre she sings " When I am laid in earth ". The ground bass on which it is built is quoted on p. 16.

Purcell gave music lessons at his home too, and wrote little pieces for his pupils which he grouped together into suites or " lessons ". They were written for the harpsichord, which looked rather like a grand piano, but instead of hammers hitting the strings they were plucked by quills. This minuet is often played. Sing it an octave lower.

Minuet from Suite No.1

" A Trumpet Tune " is quoted on p. 47, and the famous " Trumpet Voluntary," which some say is by Jeremiah Clarke and not by Purcell at all, is quoted on p. 77. Purcell wrote a good deal of ceremonial music, in his position as court composer.

A tune which he wrote for a play called " The Moor's Revenge " has been used by our modern English composer, Benjamin Britten, as a basis for his work " A Young Person's Guide to the Orchestra ", which you may have heard. Here is the tune.

Tune from "The Moor's Revenge"

Purcell lived in London all his life, and when he died, at the tragically early age of 37, he was buried in Westminster Abbey.

Exercise 111. Make a list of all the music you have heard by Purcell, and add to it whenever you hear anything else by him.

Exercise 112. What do you know about the Chapel Royal? Do you think its members were glad about the restoration of the monarchy or not?

Exercise 113. Copy the first phrase of the melody of your favourite Purcell song.

Exercise 114. Name (a) another musician; (b) a poet; (c) a writer of a famous diary; (d) a great scientist who lived at the same time as Purcell.

BACH, 1685—1750

Bach

Do you remember learning, last year, about the German composer Handel, who was born in 1685, and after travelling in Italy, settled in England under George I and II? Bach was another German composer, born in the same year, though strangely enough the two never met. Bach never left Germany—which is perhaps not surprising, as he married twice and had 20 children!

Bach and Handel's music sounds very similar to many people because they lived and wrote at the same period. But their outlook and temperament were very different. Handel was mainly a composer of operas and oratorios, and liked to build his music on a large scale, while Bach wrote mainly for the home and church, and delighted in making every vocal and instrumental part as interesting and perfect as he could.

There had been musicians, particularly organists, in the Bach family for generations. If you look in " Grove ", the standard musical dictionary, you will find 38 Bachs mentioned by name, and all related to each other! Five of these are children of the great Bach (Johann Sebastian), who all achieved fame. The Bachs lived in Thuringia, in central Germany, and used to have annual reunions, when they made music together. It is sad to think that this wonderful family has now died out.

Johann Sebastian was born in the little town of Eisenach, the home of Martin Luther. His parents died before he was 10 and he was brought up by an older married brother. He did very well at school, and was so good at music that his elder brother began to get rather jealous of him. This appears to be the reason for his being forbidden to use a book of keyboard pieces belonging to his brother. However, Johann Sebastian crept downstairs night after night and copied it out by moonlight! All his life he copied music as a means of extending his library, for music was rarely printed in those days. And quite often he ruled his own staves too—no wonder he went blind in his old age!

Bach began to earn his living by music when he was 15, first as a singer, then as a violinist and, at 18, as an organist. The organ was his favourite instrument, and during these early years he lost no opportunity of hearing other great organists, even though it might mean tramping 30 miles to do so. The greatest of them all was Buxtehude, and Bach might have taken his place when he retired if he had been willing to marry his daughter and provide a home for the old man! When he returned from visiting Buxtehude he got into trouble with the church authorities for having been so long away, and for the " new fangled " ideas he had brought back with him! They grew even more angry when he allowed a young girl to sing in the church choir! She also was a Bach, and a year later he married her and moved to a more congenial post.

When he was 23 he became the organist to the Duke of Weimar, and during the nine years he was in that town (later to be the home of the greatest German poet, Goethe) he wrote much organ and church music. Then he moved to Cöthen, where he had to conduct the court orchestra. He wrote much music for it, as well as some fine pieces for the harpsichord or clavichord.

The last 27 years of Bach's life were spent in the great town of Leipzig, where he was the music master of the choir school, and was called the " Cantor ". He was supposed to teach the boys Latin as well as music, but out of his small salary he paid someone else to do this! The boys provided the choirs for the four town churches, and Bach conducted the choir and orchestra at St. Thomas's, the most important of them. But his relations with the Headmaster, the University and the Town Council were sometimes difficult and Bach was prepared to fight for the cause of music. However, he gradually became quite famous as an organist, though not so well known as a composer, and his teaching attracted pupils from far and near.

He was happy in his home life, and proud of his family. One of his sons, Carl Philipp Emanuel, was in charge of the music at the court of Frederick the Great of Prussia, and his father went to visit him in his old age. When he arrived, Frederick the Great stopped playing his flute and cried out in delight " Gentlemen, old Bach is here!" He showed him his collection of musical instruments, particularly the new " forte-pianos " which had hammers to hit the strings. Bach did not think much of them, which is not surprising, as the hammers were not covered with felt, as they are to-day, and their tone must have been hard.

When Bach died in 1750, his sons Carl Philipp Emanuel and Johann Christoph (who was at the English Court) were more famous than he was, and his music was thought of as old fashioned. But to-day he is considered one of the greatest, if not the greatest, of all musicians. Probably old Bach himself would be surprised if he knew how much his music is known and loved to-day, over 200 years after his death.

If you think of a song, such as " All through the Night ", you will realise that it consists of a melody, usually at the top, and chords, usually underneath, making the harmony, like this:—

As long as the chords fit the tune, no-one minds whether they make a tuneful part in themselves or not. Bach sometimes wrote like this. But more often he wrote in " counterpoint ", that is, two or more equally interesting tunes, cleverly made to fit well together, like this:—

This is more interesting for the performers, and more interesting for the listener too, if he can follow the parts, but it requires greater attention. And it is more difficult to compose.

Divide your class in half and try to sing two tunes together, such as "Auld Lang Syne " and " God save the Queen ", and you will realise how they clash. A pair that happen to fit are " Three Blind Mice " and " Frère Jacques ", so try this, too. Then listen to the gay little dance in two parts, which starts like this:—

Bach wrote it for one of his sons. First the right hand skips up the doh chord, then it runs down by step while the left hand skips up, and so on. See if you can follow each part.

Your .teacher may play you two minuets which come in Dr. Carroll's " First Lessons in Bach ", Book I, Nos. 7 and 9. Try to listen to both the right and left hand parts, and see what you notice about them.

The most elaborate contrapuntal form is called " fugue ". It is all based on one short fragment of melody called a " subject ", which enters in each voice or instrument in turn, in imitation, in tonic and dominant keys alternatively. After they have all entered, the subject may be given a little rest or appear only in fragments, but it soon appears in full in another key, and finally of course, it appears at least once in the tonic key. A fugue has been humourously defined as " a piece of music in which the voices come in one by one and the listeners go out one by one ", but actually it is great fun to " spot " the subject in different parts.

Here is the subject of the fugue which occurs in the last movement of Bach's Brandenburg Concerto No. 2, for solo flute, oboe, trumpet and violin, string orchestra and harpsichord.

Sing this tune until you are quite sure you know it. Then listen to the record, and see if you can recognise it every time it comes in. You will hear it in different instruments and different keys. You will also hear bits of it at various times, but don't count these fragments. The first four entries are trumpet, oboe, violin and flute, and there are 12 entries altogether. No. 11 comes in the 'cellos, basses and harpsichord, and the piece finishes with four bars of it played by the trumpet (No. 12).

Bach had quite a number of harpsichords and clavichords in his home and used to tune them himself. To encourage a new system of tuning which made it possible to play in tune in every key, he wrote 24 preludes and fugues, one in each major and minor key. Towards the end of his life he wrote another similar set of 24, and the whole, " the 48 ", has been called " the Musician's Bible ". They are harder to follow than fugues for several *different* instruments or voices, and they are hard to play, too. But Bach also wrote easier music for keyboard instruments, such as the suites you are told about in Chapter seven.

Perhaps Bach's finest memorial is the vocal music he wrote for the church. His largest works are a fine mass in B minor and a setting of the story of Christ's Passion as told by Saint Matthew. But he also wrote many small church cantatas—there are quotations from four in this book. They all contain at least one setting of a hymn tune (called a " chorale " by the Germans) which the congregation present would know. Sometimes the setting was very elaborate and contrapuntal.

In his lighter moments Bach also wrote secular (i.e. not sacred) cantatas, such as the " Peasant Cantata " for a country jollification, and the " Coffee Cantata ", about a girl who *would* drink coffee! The following, one of Bach's most loved arias, comes from a secular cantata:—

If you are musical you will grow to love Bach's music more and more as you grow older, until you will agree with Schumann that " music owes almost as great a debt to Bach as a religion owes to its founder."

Exercise 115. Write a few lines about each of the following in relation to Bach:—Handel; Bach's eldest brother; two of Bach's sons; Buxtehude; St. Thomas's Church, Leipzig.

Exercise 116. Name three towns in which Bach lived, and write a few lines about what he did in each.

Exercise 117. What is a cantata? Name two by Bach, and copy a theme from one of them.

Exercise 118. Ask your church organist if he will play something by Bach as a voluntary next Sunday.

Exercise 119. If you are a pianist learn to play a dance by Bach. He wrote a collection of very easy keyboard pieces for his second wife, Anna Magdalena, so you should be able to manage one of those, even if you have not been learning very long. If you are not a pianist or the pieces are too difficult, then learn to sing the minuet which is quoted on p. 32, and which also belongs to the Anna Magdalena book.

Exercise 120. There are 17 named compositions by Bach quoted in this book. Find them all and make a list of them. Tick the ones you have actually heard, and name the three you like best.

HAYDN, 1732—1809

Haydn

Just as one refers to Bach and Handel in one breath, so one couples the names of Haydn and Mozart. But whereas Bach and Handel were born in the same year, Haydn was a generation older than Mozart, though he lived on for 18 years after Mozart's death. Bach and Handel were both Germans. Haydn and Mozart were both Austrians, and, unlike Bach and Handel, they not only met but became great friends, each admiring and emulating the works of the other.

The great Bach was still alive when Haydn was born, in 1732, and Central Europe still consisted mainly of wealthy people like princes, counts and bishops, and poor people who served them. Joseph Haydn was one of the poor people. He was born in a small Austrian village where the simple peasants sang cheerful folk songs and danced gay dances. His father was a wheelwright, and his mother had been a cook, and he was one of a family of twelve. Joseph might have become a wheelwright just like his father, and the musical world been much poorer, if he had not happened to possess a good voice. This got him into the Vienna choir school, the same one that Schubert was to attend over half a century later. Schubert, you may remember, was a dreamy youth who was always wanting music paper so that he could compose. But Haydn, though he too wanted to compose, was a jolly fellow, full of mischief, and many tales are told of his pranks, such as climbing some scaffolding on the Emperor's palace, Schonbrunn, and cutting off the pigtail of another boy, for all the boys wore wigs. The choir master tolerated him because he was the chief solo singer, but when, at 16, his voice broke, he was dismissed and his younger brother took the solos in his place.

Haydn might perhaps have gone back to his native village, but by now he loved Vienna and its musical life. So he managed to rent an attic and struggled to support himself by doing any odd jobs that came along. He worked for a wig maker; accompanied for a singing teacher with the odd name of Porpora for whom he also acted as valet, mending his clothes and blacking his boots in exchange for composition lessons; and taught, sang and played at all sorts of functions. He came across the sonatas of Carl Philipp Emanuel Bach, who was writing in a simple, less contrapuntal style than that of his father, and learnt how to compose by using them as his models. He also bought text books with his hard earned money, and studied them on his own, as best he could.

On one occasion he was invited to stay at a large country house, to make music. He found a small orchestra there, so at once set to work to write music for it, thus producing his first symphony. There were also two good violinists, a violist and a 'cellist, so Haydn wrote music for them too, producing string quartets, which were then something rather new. Haydn loved the minuet, and the earliest of these symphonies and quartets often had five movements, with two minuets. The tune of the first minuet from Op. 1, No. 1 is quoted on p. 58.

At last, when he was nearly 29, his great chance came. He was appointed music master (Kapellmeister) to the great Prince Esterhazy. Most wealthy musical people kept a small orchestra in their household. But Prince Esterhazy was so wealthy that he wore diamonds instead of buttons on his dress uniform and could entertain hundreds of guests in his enormous palace, which was as big as Versailles. And he was so musical that he kept a large orchestra permanently employed, had an opera house in his grounds as well as a marionette theatre, and often played himself, on a strange string instrument called a baryton.

In a sense, Haydn was no more than a servant. But he did not mind, for he was given a summer house all to himself, in which to compose; then, after getting his musicians to copy out the parts, he could always try his symphonies out on the orchestra and change anything that he thought was not quite right. In this way he learnt what combinations of instruments made the best symphony orchestra, how best to write for them, what musical forms were the most satisfying, and so on. Every orchestral composer since Haydn owes a debt to Esterhazy for giving Haydn this opportunity to become the " Father of the Symphony ", as all have learnt from what he did.

Of course, life was rather dull. The Prince's palace was in the country and at times the orchestra got restive, and wanted to return to their families in Vienna. Haydn had married a daughter of the wig maker and had found her such a shrew that he had no desire to return. But, for the sake of the orchestra, he wrote the " Farewell Symphony ", in which, in the last movement, the players stopped playing one by one, and stole off the platform, until only two were left playing. Fortunately the Prince, like Haydn, had a sense of humour and took the hint.

Haydn wrote over a hundred symphonies. Many of them have nick-names, like the " Clock ", in which the accompaniment of the slow movement sounds just like the ticking of a clock (the theme is quoted on p. 59), or the " Surprise ", where the trumpets and the drums come in unexpectedly in the slow movement. Haydn said, with a chuckle. " There, all the women will scream!" This theme is quoted on p. 25. The bang occurs at the end of the first half when it is played for the second time, but nowadays we are used to loud bangs, even in quiet slow movements, so we hardly notice it. Haydn's sense of humour comes out in other places, too, as, e.g. in the sudden pauses in the minuet from the ". London " symphony in D, the themes from which are quoted on p. 68. He remained at heart a simple minded peasant who delighted in good tunes, gaiety and humour. The finales of his symphonies have jolly tunes, rather like the folk songs and dances he heard in his village as a boy (see pp. 13 and 20.) Most of his religious music is cheerful too. He once said " At the thought of God my heart leaps for joy, and I cannot help my music doing the same."

After a time, Haydn's fame as a composer spread all over Europe. Out of loyalty to Esterhazy, Haydn refused the invitations he received to visit other countries, but when at last the Prince died, leaving him a handsome pension, he came to England twice, at the invitation of the famous violinist, Saloman. He wrote 12 symphonies for Saloman's concerts, including the " Surprise " (quotation p. 25), the " Clock " (quotations pp. 13, 59 and 66), the

" Military " (quotation p. 43), and the " London " (quotations pp. 20 and 68). Haydn was nearly 60 at his first visit and he did not like the London street noises or fogs. But he received many invitations to dine, and Oxford made him a Doctor of Music and performed his " Oxford Symphony ". He played at court, was presented with 6 pairs of stockings embroidered with favourite tunes from his music, and earned over £2,000.

He heard Handel's oratorio, the Messiah, and was so impressed by it that he went home with a poem based on the bible and Milton's " Paradise Lost " to set to music in the same way. His fine oratorio, " The Creation " was the result. This work opens with a wonderful picture of Chaos, containing queer, shifting, chaotic harmonies and modulations. You should hear this, and also No. 2 " In the beginning God created the heaven and the earth " with its wonderful burst of sound, on the chord of C major, at the words " and there was *light* ". Haydn, at the last performance he attended, pointed a hand upwards at this moment and said " It came from thence!" Haydn enjoys describing the creation of the winds, thunder, lightning and snow in recitative in No. 4, and tells delightfully of the creation of the birds and beasts in Part II. " With verdure clad " is a lovely spring-like soprano aria which begins like this:—

The Creation. With verdure clad

With verd-ure clad the fields ap-pear, De-light-ful to— the rav-ished sense

Part I ends with a fine chorus " The Heavens are telling ":—

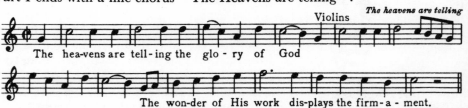

Violins   *The heavens are telling*

The hea-vens are tell-ing the glo-ry of God

The won-der of His work dis-plays the firm-a-ment.

Haydn was also impressed by our British National Anthem, so went back to Austria and wrote " The Emperor's Hymn ", which you know as a hymn tune, and which he incorporated in the " Emperor " quartet. It is quoted on pp. 40 and 69.

When Haydn lay dying, at the age of 77, Vienna was being besieged by Napoleon's armies, and a shot fell near his garden. But it is touching to learn that, after the city was occupied by the French, one of Napoleon's officers came into his room and sang " In Native Worth " from " The Creation ", as a mark of esteem, and French soldiers took part in the guard of honour at his funeral.

Haydn was affectionately known as " Papa Haydn ", and was loved by everyone. But he was father in another way too, father of the symphony and the quartet, and all symphonic and chamber music writers owe a great debt to him.

Exercise 121. Give some of the reasons why Haydn is important in the history of music.

Exercise 122. Name four of Haydn's symphonies, and copy a theme from one of them.

Exercise 123. Write a few lines about each of the following, in relation to Haydn:—(a) The Vienna Choir School; (b) Esterhazy; (c) Mozart; (d) Saloman; (e) Handel; (f) Napoleon.

Exercise 124. Take any opportunity you may get to hear a Haydn Symphony either at a concert or on the radio, or television.

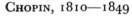

CHOPIN, 1810—1849

Chopin

A year after Haydn died, in French-occupied Vienna, Chopin was born in Poland. While he was a child, Napoleon, having almost conquered Europe, was thrown back from Russia, and finally defeated at the battle of Waterloo, in 1815.

Poland was on the side of France in these troublous times, and there was a close and friendly link between the two countries. Napoleon's army wintered in Poland in 1806, and this was the year that Chopin's father, a Frenchman who had come to Poland some years before to work for a snuff manufacturer, married a Polish girl in Warsaw, and left the snuff manufacturer to become a teacher of French.

Frederic, the only son, was born in 1810 and soon showed such musical gifts as to be called a second Mozart. He played a piano concerto in public when he was 9, went to the Warsaw College of Music at 14, and published his first piano piece, a rondo, at 15. He was particularly good at improvising on the piano, and he enjoyed acting, too, when he got the chance. He was also very interested in Polish literature.

When he was 20 he embarked on the career of a concert pianist and began to tour Europe, little thinking that he was never to see his beloved Poland again. But a year later Poland was occupied by the Russians, and thenceforth he was an exile. He was so angry and despairing when he heard of the Russian occupation that he wrote the tempestuous " Revolutionary " study, Op. 10, No. 12 in C minor, which you will enjoy hearing on the gramophone.

At first he made Vienna his centre, because it had been, and still was the home of so many famous musicians. There he was recognised as a fine pianist and a good composer, though some people thought his playing was too quiet and delicate. It was at this time that Schumann, writing in his music journal, exclaimed " Hats off, gentlemen! a genius !

In a short while he moved to Paris, which became his home for the rest of his life—though he nearly went to America when things were not going well! However, after playing at the home of the wealthy Rothschilds, he began to get more pupils and engagements. He was particularly popular at the " Soirées " which the wealthy Parisians used to hold, when admiring ladies would cluster round the piano and ask him to play his waltzes. He was poetic-looking and frail, and that, too, excited their sympathetic interest. One of these ladies, who was a well-known novelist and gave herself the pen-name of George Sand, took pity on him and took him, with her children, to winter in the island of Majorca in the Mediterranean, in an effort to improve his health. Although she often wore men's clothes, she was a motherly woman and did her best for Chopin, but the dreaded tuberculosis had laid its hold on him, the conditions in which they lived, in a disused monastery, were very primitive, and they had appalling weather. It was romantic enough and very beautiful, but the monastery lay in the shadow of mountains till noon and again after 3 o'clock, when the mists came down and the wind howled round the cloisters and poor Chopin shivered and coughed.

Chopin wrote his 24 preludes while he was here. Some of these are very short—though none of them is a prelude to anything else. No. 7 (16 bars) is built entirely on ♩ | ♩.♪♩ ♩ | ♩ ‖. Clap this rhythm quietly while your teacher plays it. No. 20 (13 bars) is again built entirely on one rhythm (♩ ♩ ♩.♩). Sing the tune while your teacher plays it.

Prelude 15 is said to be the result of a quarrel with George Sand, when Chopin was feeling very miserable and the rain fell relentlessly. It has been nicknamed the " Raindrop " prelude. One note, sometimes written as A♭ sometimes as G♯, is monotonously repeated, like raindrops, nearly all the way through.

Chopin and George Sand returned to Paris, and did not come to Majorca again, but spent their winters in Paris, and their summers at George Sand's chateau in central France.

They quarrelled and separated seven years later, when Chopin was 37, and this made Chopin very unhappy.

The following year, 1848, France had another revolution, and Chopin fled to England, where he was received into the houses of the wealthy, and somehow managed to give a concert tour, travelling as far as Manchester, Glasgow, and Edinburgh. But he often had to be carried upstairs, he was so weak, and he returned to Paris so ill that he died very soon afterwards.

When he left Poland he had been given a silver box containing Polish earth by his fellow students, and the contents were strewn over his coffin at the the funeral.

The other composers you have been told about so far all wrote many different kinds of music. But Chopin was a specialist—he only wrote piano music. It was piano music of a kind that had never been heard before, however, wonderfully delicate at times, fiery at others, making effective use of the recently invented sustaining pedal, and, in a word, being very " pianistic ". The delicacy and refinement were French characteristics, while the fiery qualities were Polish. The mazurkas and polonaises mentioned in Chapter VII were Polish dances, and Chopin frequently gave concerts to help the many Polish refugees in Paris, who received much sympathy from the French. The waltz originated in Austria, but Chopin's " Valses de Salon " were much loved by the Parisian ladies.

He met an Irishman called Field who had written dreamy kinds of pieces he called " nocturnes ", and Chopin wrote 19 of them, of which the best known begins thus. Notice that it is in compound four time.

He also wrote two sets of studies, which are not only difficult technically, but beautiful as well. The " Revolutionary " study has already been mentioned. You would. enjoy the " Black Note " study, which has quick triplets in the right hand entirely on the black notes, and Op. 10, No. 3, a quiet one which begins like this:—

His pieces were mostly short and were grouped into sets, but he wrote three piano sonatas, and the slow movement from one of them is a funeral march which was played at his own funeral. The first part is built on the slow rhythm ♩ ♩.♪♩ ♩ and the middle, trio, section has a lovely consoling tune:—

Chopin was, indeed, the poet of the piano, and his music is beloved by pianists all over the world.

Exercise 125. How did political events in Poland and France affect Chopin?

Exercise 126. Name as many different kinds of piano works that Chopin wrote as possible.

Exercise 127. Copy your favourite melody by Chopin.

Exercise 128. Encourage your pianist friends to play you some pieces by Chopin.

BRAHMS, 1833—1897

Brahms

For our next composer, Brahms, we turn once more to Germany, though, like the German, Beethoven, he settled in Vienna, the home of so many great musicians.

He was born in Hamburg, when Chopin was 23. There were a number of minor revolutions in Europe while he was a youth, but, after that, he lived in a comparatively peaceful half-century.

Like Mozart and Beethoven, he was the son of a musician, but whereas Mozart's and Beethoven's fathers were court musicians, Brahms's father lived in a town, and played the double bass and the horn in a theatre.

His father saw to it that Johannes had a good musical training, and at the age of 20 he began a tour of Europe with a Hungarian violinist, with whom he played Hungarian dances. Later, Brahms arranged many of these dances for orchestra and as piano duets, and they are very popular today. No. 5 starts like this:—

Hungarian Dance No.5

The great violinist, Joachim, heard him play at one of their concerts, and befriended him and introduced him to Schumann. Schumann helped him, as he had helped Chopin, by writing most enthusiastically about him in his musical journal, and he and his wife, Clara, became his greatest friends, calling him "the Young Eagle". When Schumann had to be taken to an asylum, Brahms helped Clara and her children in every way he could, and the warm friendship continued throughout their lives.

When he was 21 he accepted a position as a court composer, like that of Haydn, and he held it for four years. He had a choir to conduct, and this perhaps started his interest in choral music. He wrote some lovely songs for female voices, horns and harp, and his requiem mass, inspired by the death of Schumann and of his Mother, is a very fine work indeed. It does not use the words of the traditional Latin mass, as does Mozart's, but consists of German texts, taken from the Bible. The following lovely chorus is available on records :—

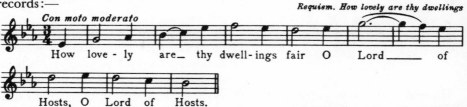

Requiem. How lovely are thy dwellings

How love-ly are_ thy dwell-ings fair O Lord_____ of Hosts, O Lord of Hosts.

After a short period in Switzerland, Brahms settled in Vienna, spending the last 35 years of his life there. Although he held no full-time appointment, he conducted the Viennese Choral Society, and soon became acknowledged as Vienna's chief composer. Vienna was famous for light music as well as serious, and you have probably heard of Johann Strauss, who wrote " The Blue Danube". Brahms loved light music, too, and there are two waltzes of his quoted on pp. 38 and 66. When he was asked to write something in Frau Strauss's autograph album he wrote a few bars of " The Blue Danube " and added " Unfortunately *not* by your devoted friend Johannes Brahms ".

After settling in Vienna, Brahms lived a very uneventful life. He never married, though he loved children and they loved playing with him, particularly the Schumann children, for whom he wrote the songs quoted on pp. 41, 48 and 52. He rapidly became a benevolent looking, bearded old bachelor, delighting in simple life and wearing old clothes. He was asked to conduct a series of London Philharmonic Concerts, and receive an honorary degree from Cambridge, but he refused because he would have had to wear his best clothes all the time!

Unlike Chopin, he was interested in many branches of music, and he wrote in almost every medium except opera. Following the example of Schubert and Schumann, he wrote over 200 songs: love songs such as his two serenades;

songs of nature such as " To the Nightingale ", " May Night ", and " In Summer Fields "; and songs of the folk song type such as the well-known " Blacksmith ". Sing it while your teacher plays it, noticing the hammer-like leaps in the tune and the accompaniment.

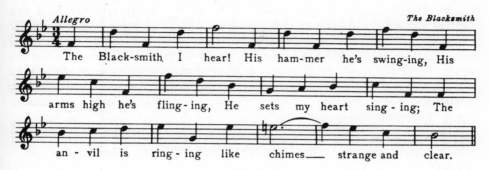

He was also a fine piano composer, giving his pieces such indefinite titles as intermezzo and rhapsody. A popular rhapsody starts like this:—

He left a wealth of chamber music which you will enjoy as you grow older, and some magnificent orchestral music. He much admired Beethoven's nine symphonies, and his first symphony—which he took 14 years to write—was hailed by enthusiastic friends as " the Tenth ". (You learnt a tune from it last year.) He wrote four great symphonies, two fine piano concertos and a lovely violin concerto. All his orchestral music is finely constructed, and full of rich colour and beautiful tunes, though the movements are rather long for you to follow, as yet.

The theme from his popular " Variations on a theme of Haydn " is quoted on p. 36. In lighter vein he wrote an " Academic Festival Overture " for an honorary degree he received from Breslau University. It is full of jolly student songs such as the following. Sing the tunes, and then see if you can recognise them when they come on the record.

Brahms's fame as a composer spread all over the world. He was given the freedom of his native city, Hamburg, and when he died in Vienna he was buried in the same cemetery as Beethoven and Schubert.

Exercise 129. Name five works by Brahms, and write a few lines about one of them.

Exercise 130. Copy your favourite tune by Brahms, then learn it from memory.

Exercise 131. Make a list of all the songs by Brahms that you know.

Exercise 132. Give the names of five German composers, three Austrian, two English, one Polish and one Norwegian.

Exercise 133. Name four great symphony writers, three great German song writers, two composers who wrote a requiem mass, and three composers of chamber music.

Exercise 134. If you made a time chart of last year's composers, add this year's composers to it.